# THE Quilts of Tennessee

*Images of Domestic Life Prior to 1930*

## Bets Ramsey and Merikay Waldvogel

PHOTOGRAPHY BY David Luttrell

RUTLEDGE HILL PRESS

*Nashville, Tennessee*

Published in Nashville, Tennessee, by Rutledge Hill Press, Inc., 513 Third Avenue South, Nashville, Tennessee 37210.

*Design:* Harriette Bateman
*Typography:* ProtoType Graphics, Inc.

**Library of Congress Cataloging-in-Publication Data**

Ramsey, Bets, 1923-
  The quilts of Tennessee.

  Includes index.
  1. Quilts—Tennessee—Catalogs.  2. Quiltmakers—Tennessee—Biography.
2. Waldvogel, Merikay, 1947-
II. Title.
NK9112.R36  1986      746.9′7′09768       86-14263
ISBN 0-934395-30-6

3 4 5 6 7 8 9 10 — 92 91 90 89

Printed in Hong Kong

*for* PAUL AND JERRY

## [1] BURSTING STAR (Blazing Star)

*Maker:* Timexenia M. Morris Roper.
  Stewart County, 1861-1865.
*Lender:* Emmett Allan Roper, Jr.,
  grandson.
*Pieced:* 84″ x 82½″; cotton: assorted colors
  with black, yellow-orange home-dyed
  tobacco sacks; tan and pink print back;
  edge turned to front; allover double row
  shell quilting in black thread.

Mrs. Roper made this quilt for her son
Emmett, as she made other quilts for his
twin brother and older brother. She saved
her husband's tobacco sacks and dyed them
to add a bright color to the star quilt. The
Star of Bethlehem has had many
interpretations, but this one, set among
many tiny twinkling stars, truly
demonstrates its magnitude.

For detail see page 13.

# Contents

# Illustrations

# *Preface*

Our study of Tennessee quilts began some years ago. For me it began in 1971 when I first encountered a group of family quilts as I was doing research for a graduate school project. Merikay moved to Knoxville in 1977 with a small collection of quilts and, wanting to make additions, sought out regional quiltmakers and their work. Our paths crossed. We found a common bond in our admiration for country quilts and oddities of design. It was the beginning of our collaboration in workshops, seminars, and exhibitions. In late 1983 we decided to undertake a survey of Tennessee quilts.

We arranged to visit several locations in the state in order to photograph and examine quilts made in Tennessee before 1930. We suggested, in advance, that quilt owners bring relevant genealogical material and photographs. The survey included owner and maker information, quilt provenance, detailed study of each quilt's physical characteristics, and photographs. Research of pattern identification was not done at the survey site, but at a later time. We hoped through the study to formulate a profile of Tennessee quilts and denote regional and historical differences.

Katy Christopherson, consultant to the Kentucky Quilt Project, provided help and offered advice as we devised our survey form. Profiting from the experience of the Kentucky group, we designed our two-page form. It was arranged to help us gather as much relevant information as was possible within the time limits of a busy quilt day.

As we began scheduling documentation days, we were fortunate to be able to recruit enthusiastic, reliable local coordinators. Each was responsible for securing a suitable location, arranging publicity, finding volunteers, preparing the site, and, in some cases, providing lunch. We held thirty quilt days in twenty-two locations across the state. More than 1000 people were involved. Facilities were generously provided by museums, churches, schools and universities, a bank, community and utility buildings, farm agencies, courthouses, senior centers, and a visitors' center.

We began our survey without financial support and immediately applied for grants, without success. Our project did not fit the guidelines of any state or private agency to which we applied. As it hap-

*"Yes, these quilts just talk back to you, don't they?"*
—Unidentified antique dealer at Nashville flea market

pened, we managed to stay solvent through many small and some large donations, speakers' fees, occasional paid expenses, and numerous five-dollar contributions from owners for a copy of their quilt's documentation. The project's success was due to the enthusiastic response of its many participants.

A typical quilt day began with the owner signing the register and receiving an identification number for each quilt. Then she or he was interviewed for family history and quilt-related stories. The quilt was delivered to the photography area where a Polaroid picture was taken and immediately attached to the form. Two full and two close-up slides were then taken and, as required, additional shots of detail or the back of the quilt. Meanwhile the owner viewed slides from previous quilt days and chatted with other quilt owners. Finally the quilt reached the examining table where it was measured and studied for detail of construction, pattern, fabric, age, technique, condition, and quality of design. The historic value of family quilts and their preservation was emphasized; upon leaving, each participant received a guidesheet about quilt care. Our quilt days were busy—sometimes hectic—with scarcely time for lunch, but they were always rewarding.

Volunteer training sessions were held an hour prior to the opening of each quilt day. After assignments were made, the operation began. While a few volunteers interviewed owners, many more carried quilts in and out to be photographed, since outdoor light gave the best results. Helpers hung and removed quilts from the metal hanging-frame, returned quilts to the documentation area, and assisted with measurements and descriptions. In a word, volunteers were the heart

Locations of documented quilts of known origins.

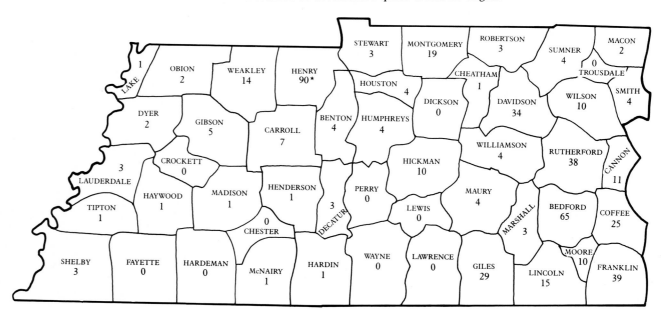

of the quilt days, providing hundreds of hours of valuable service. Our own responsibilities were divided, with Merikay overseeing volunteers and photography while I worked on documentation and research of patterns.

When we began the Tennessee quilt study, we expected to find many exceptional quilts of high quality and many more ordinary quilts of practical value. We hoped there would be a few unorthodox quilts as well. We did, indeed, find all of these; but we found something more. As we gave our intense concentration and study to the quilts, we found the lives of the quilters and their families and descendants becoming equally important. Some glimpses of the history of a state and its people were revealed as we examined the evidence of the past.

We have learned much about the quiltmaking traditions of Tennessee through our survey, and we truly appreciate the diversity and beauty of the work. Even more, we cherish the lives of the quiltmakers who put something of themselves into every quilt.

Although we surveyed 1,425 quilts, we know that many more were not brought to the quilt days. Our limited sampling and profile of Tennessee quilts offers an addition to the collected body of information from other state projects. Through these studies quilt owners, collectors and historians can make comparisons and trace the continuity of quilt patterns and styles. They can find relationships to social, economic, political and religious circumstances. The similarities and differences, the history and family lore, and the artistry and craftsmanship are combined to give a fascinating record of human life.

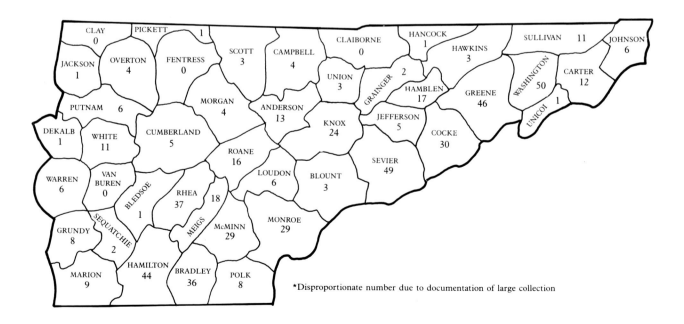

*Disproportionate number due to documentation of large collection

# The Tennessee Quilt Exhibit

## EXHIBITION SCHEDULE

American Museum of Science and Energy
Oak Ridge
November 1—December 31, 1986

Rose Center
Morristown
February 2—March 15, 1987

George T. Hunter Museum of Art
Chattanooga
April 5—May 17, 1987

Nathanael Greene Museum
Greeneville
June 4–21, 1987

Carroll Reece Museum
Johnson City
July 1—August 16, 1987

Knoxville Museum of Art
Knoxville
October 23—November 1, 1987

Memphis Pink Palace
Memphis
November 21, 1987—January 24, 1988

Tennessee State Museum
Nashville
July 7—August 21, 1988

## COUNTIES WHERE EXHIBITION QUILTS WERE MADE

BEDFORD
*Basket Quilt*
*Log Cabin in Squares and Diamonds*
*Peddler's Quilt*
*Sunburst*

BRADLEY
*Cockscomb & Currants*

COCKE
*Friendship*

DAVIDSON
*Red and Green Star (Rolling Star)*

FRANKLIN
*Wheel of Fortune*

GIBSON
*The World's Fair Quilt (Golden Splendor Variation)*

GREENE
*Tree of Life*
*Whig Rose*

HAMILTON
*Crazy Quilt*

HENRY
*Milky Way*
*Star in a Basket*

HICKMAN
*Blue Patchwork Cross (Unequal Nine Patch)*

JOHNSON
*Rose Tree*

KNOX
*Brick*
*Linsey Quilt*
*Log Cabin (Pig Pen)*

LINCOLN
*Martha Washington's Flower Garden*
*Worsted Quilt (Dresden Plate)*

McMINN
*Trip Around the World, My Hard Times Quilt*

MEIGS
*Rose of Sharon*
*Schoolhouse*
*Winding Rose*

MONROE
*Crown of Thorns (New York Beauty)*

MOORE
*Radiant Star*

MORGAN
*Sampler of Blocks*

RHEA
*Double Irish Chain*
*Feathered Star*
*Trentham Quilt*

RUTHERFORD
*Bible Verses Quilt*
*Dutch Tulips*
*Soule College Quilt*

ROANE
*Basket of Scraps*

SEVIER
*String*

SULLIVAN
*Jefferson Rose*

STEWART
*Bursting Star (Blazing Star)*

The following individuals have graciously lent their quilts for the Tennessee Quilt Exhibit.

Mary Johnson Browning
Bettye J. Broyles
Charlotte Haymore Clark
Elyssa Hood Clayton
Emily Daniel Cox
Anna Lillard Donelson
Barbara Tunnell Hale
James Howard Hall
Robert B. Hicks, III
Terry Irwin
Evelyn Grant Knight
Polly LaFollette
Jerry Ledbetter
Mary K. Morelock Ledford
Mildred Locke
Lorene Little Mantooth
McMinn County Living Heritage Museum
    & J. Howard Hornsby, Jr., and family
McMinn County Living Heritage Museum
    & Mrs. W. A. Shadow and
    her daughter, Muriel S. Mayfield

Ellen Goodrich Morgan
Kathryn Susong Neas ·
Newport-Cocke County Museum
    & Eldridge Baxter Smelcer,
    Ola Baxter Thomas,
    Willie Ruth Baxter Williams,
    Judy Baxter Wright,
    and Jeffery Baxter Wright
Judy Pratt
Carolyn Hodge Rogers
Emmett Allan Roper, Jr.
Martha Boulton Shelton
Sue Curtis Smith
Mildred Elizabeth Rawls Stovall
Tennessee State Museum
    & Dr. and Mrs. Robert Haley, Jr.
Sarah Thomas
Family of Randolph M. and JoAn T. Trentham
Mary Heiskell Wasson
Jeanne Gilmore Webb

# Explanatory Notes

Quilt names are those given by owners or in regional use and are not always those in general use. Alternate names are given in parentheses.

Quilting thread is white unless otherwise noted.

Batting is cotton unless otherwise noted.

Quilts were selected with certain considerations: strong visual image, known provenance, geographic location, representation of survey categories, innovation, and historical significance.

Length and width measurements were taken through the center section of each quilt.

**[2] DUTCH TULIPS.**

*Maker:* Mother of Mrs. Sharber.
 Rutherford County, circa 1890.
*Lender:* Mildred Locke.
*Applique:* 84¾″ x 77½″; cotton: green,
 red, yellow-orange on white; muslin
 back; red binding on the straight; quilted
 by the piece in concentric rows,
 diamonds, and diagonal rows with red,
 green, and white thread.

The maker was very skillful in using a
straight machine-stitch to applique all parts
of this dramatic quilt. Her placement of the
blocks, with the four flowers in the center,
is ingenious.

# Introduction

Quilts—layers of fabric and filling—are not new, nor did they originate in America. Along with quilted bed furnishings and clothing, they have been used in various cultures and locations for hundreds of years. Derived from European models of the seventeenth and eighteenth centuries, American quilts have acquired distinct qualities and characteristics during 200 years of development. Now they are being emulated in Africa, Europe, and the Orient as a form of Western needlework, even though quilting was an ancient practice in some of those same places.

Household inventories, bills of lading, letters, and diaries from America's colonial period indicate that blankets and bed rugs were the standard bed coverings of the time. English and French furnishing styles were copied in the more affluent homes, and the few quilts listed in inventories were classed as luxury items. But soon individual adaptations and inventions supplanted European patterns, and the American quilt industry began to flourish at the time of the Revolutionary War.

Quiltmaking was practiced in the majority of homes on all economic levels during the nineteenth century. Elegant, refined work continued to be produced, but more often colorful patchwork was made for everyday use. With a largely rural population dependent on local resources, quiltmaking was usually the work of the female members of the household. It was practical work, but it also gave pleasure and satisfaction to the makers and brought beauty into the surroundings.

An occasional quilting bee was a festive occasion, but more often quilting was practiced by family groups working in the routine of daily living. Homemakers in agricultural families seldom had a free day. While some group quilt gatherings took place in the nineteenth century, it was in the early twentieth century when women began attending more social meetings that church quilting groups became most popular.

1

**[3] WINDING ROSE.**

*Maker:* Aunt Eliza "Liza," slave of family of Tennie McKenzie Marler.
*Signed:* "L. McK."
Goodfield Community, Meigs County, circa 1860.
*Lender:* Oscar L. Davis, grandson of Tennie McKenzie Marler.
*Applique:* 90½"x 81"; cotton: red, yellow-orange, rose print, brown print (faded green); white handwoven back; red binding on the straight; quilting is allover touching circles ¾" in diameter, possibly a thimble outline.

The design character seems related to European embroidery motifs of the late seventeenth and eighteenth centuries.

It is known through records and family accounts that during the period of slavery some women trained household help to quilt. Some splendid slave-made quilts have been carefully preserved and cherished by their owners. A few generous owners have donated these quilts to museums where they may be appreciated by a wider audience than within a private collection. After Emancipation, having acquired quilting skills, black women made quilts for themselves with whatever scraps they could gather and in whatever form they chose. Unfortuntately, few of their nineteenth-century utility quilts seem to remain because they wore out in everyday use.

Since almost every household has had quilts at one time and the majority of individuals share some knowledge of them, the quilt has been called America's most available art form. People relate warmly to quilts. They remember incidents from the past and often associate family memories with quilts. People have an understanding of how a quilt is used and how it is made. They can enjoy the colors and design without having to search for meaning, as they might at a painting exhibition.

A combination of factors contributes to the firm entrenchment of quilts in the lives of Americans. Practicality is a major reason for quilt production and popularity. While quilts made from all-new material can be quite costly, those made from scraps are considered economical, therefore "good." A quilt made from scrap material is cheaper than a purchased blanket. A quilt has a use; time spent doing practical work is not time wasted, especially in the preparation of bedding for a dowry. The Puritan and pioneer habits still apply.

There are esthetic and psychological rewards associated with quiltmaking. A quilt gives pleasure. To touch a quilt brings feelings of warmth and appreciation. The thought and planning required to produce a quilt provide the mind with healthy activity. The act of sewing itself is soothing and restful. As the work progresses, the maker experiences satisfaction and finds great reward in the completed product. The color and pattern of a quilt brighten the house and delight the eye. Through the many stages of making a quilt, a woman is creating a lasting statement of herself. If a quilt is a gift, both the giver and the recipient establish a bond through expression and acceptance of appreciation.

In a mechanical age, a quilt carries a symbolic message. It can be a reminder of people, places, or the past, a tie with one's ancestors. It gives a sense of belonging. It is a part of one's most intimate life, from birth to death. A quilt is basic to life.

Not all periods of our history have been active times for quiltmakers. Responses to economics, politics, and social events have brought about periods of greater or lesser involvement. For some reason interest seems to accelerate after major wars, and such was the case in the 1960s when there was renewed activity in several fiber arts. By 1971, when Jonathan Holstein and Gail van der Hoof exhibited their quilts at the Whitney Museum, a quilt revival was in progress. The exhibition promoted quilts as visual art forms and raised them from the classification of domestic art. The show caught the fancy of the media and articles on quilts began to appear in numerous publications. From that time on hundreds of new quilters have become enthusiastic practitioners, and quilt collecting has become a popular pursuit.

The *Wall Street Journal* has noted the effect the quilting industry has brought to the marketplace. There has been a proliferation of quilting products, publications, guilds, seminars, study groups, and investment by collectors. Perhaps it is the innate desire to touch something pleasant, to experience the tactile quality of soft fabric, which has been intensified by the cold hardness of computers and machines.

The search for meaning and history in quiltmaking is relevant if the present phenomenon is to be understood. From the Kentucky Heritage Quilt Project on, various state and regional groups are engaged in documenting quilts and recording their findings. Each quilt and each quilt owner add another bit of substance to the story. From the Tennessee study, and others like it, will come images of everyday life in America of a time now past. When the parts are joined together, we will know the history of America's quilts and quiltmakers.

# A SAMPLING OF *Tennessee Quilts*

The great migration from Virginia, Maryland, Pennsylvania, and the North which began in the late 1760s ultimately resulted in the settling of that wilderness section of the North Carolina Territory known as Tennessee. Earlier attempts at colonization had been repulsed by the Indians, but eventually treaties and land purchases allowed movement into the area. In 1777 Washington County, consisting of almost the entire present state of Tennessee, was established, with Jonesborough as the county seat. By June 1796, the rugged territory had entered the Union as the sixteenth state, Tennessee.

Tennessee! The word has a lilt and a tune. It was derived from the name for an Indian town, Tanase, which is thought to mean "beloved town." Other Indian names for towns, counties, and rivers are found throughout the state and serve as reminders of the past. Many Tennesseans today are proud to claim Indian ancestry.

Buffalo and Indian trails and rivers provided the only means of transportation for early arrivals to the state. As part of North Carolina's plan to establish a settlement at Nashville, James Robertson led a party overland from lower Virginia through the Cumberland Gap, while his associate, John Donelson, chose the river route. The flatboat journey from East Tennessee was hazardous and costly. The Donelson party endured hostile Indians, river rapids and whirlpools, bitter-cold weather, sickness, inadequate supplies, and loss of lives and goods. When Robertson failed to meet the group near Muscle Shoals for a shortened final journey by land, Donelson's party was forced to continue the roundabout water route up the Ohio and down the Cumberland rivers.[1]

More and more people came to Tennessee seeking land and greater opportunities in the mountains, plateaus, and valleys. They were mainly English, Scottish, Irish, and German, with a few French and Dutch. Few Negroes were among them. The settlers brought with them major necessities, a few cherished possessions, and their family customs and backgrounds. Once on the land, the men cleared forests

*"I have no plan to ever begin another quilt . . . as there is nothing more to accomplish. . . . Maybe now I will start an afgan or go into politics."*
—Letter from Lillian Jackson Jones to her sister after her quilt was judged "Best quilt in all 48 states and U.S. Territories"

5

to make fields. The logs were used for houses and barns, and later for schools and churches. The women fed and clothed the family while the men made shelters.

Frontier life was demanding. Strong determination was needed to make the wilderness into a civilized community. Large families provided extra help for field work but placed heavy burdens on the women who reared them. Women's lives were especially hard, with domestic chores seemingly having no end. Some pioneer women have said it was their quiltmaking that kept them sane during grim years and brought some measure of comfort and joy.

One of the landmarks on the Holston River entry route is the Old Deery Inn at Blountville. It was built by William Deery in 1795 from an unfinished log house and adjacent store purchased from Walter James. The store is thought to have been built in 1785. Deery called it his "mansion and store building with accommodations for travellers." Andrew Jackson,[2] James K. Polk, Andrew Johnson, the Marquis de Lafayette, and Prince Louis Philippe are claimed as guests. Between the inn and the owner's comfortable rooms was a combination store and post office. The store was operated largely on the barter system. In one corner of the store there is a trap door in the floor where feathers brought in for trade were dumped into a sack below. In due time a feather bed was available for purchase or trade.

The inn remained in almost continuous operation until about 1930 and was acquired later by Judge and Mrs. Joseph A. Caldwell. The house is furnished in keeping with its past. All the beds in the Old Deery Inn are covered with splendid quilts. An applique Rose of Sharon quilt is on the tall four-poster bed in the guest room. It was made in the area about 1830 from an extremely popular pattern of the time. A similar quilt of the same period is exhibited in nearby Emory and Henry College.[3]

6

[5] JEFFERSON ROSE.

*Maker:* Barbara Ford and her sisters.
  Fordtown, Sullivan County, 1849.
*Lender:* Barbara Tunnell Hale,
  granddaughter.
*Applique:* 81″ x 61½″; cotton: green, pink,
  yellow, and faded green on a white
  background; white cotton back; edge has
  front turned to back; quilting is by the
  piece in the block, stars in the
  background, and five rows of leaves in
  the plain blocks. Quilting thread is
  white, red, and dark green.

Barbara Ford was born in 1829; she made
the quilt before her marriage to Isaac
Tunnell. The quilt was quilted by Barbara
and her sisters. The family treasured the
quilt, which was never put on a bed unless
the minister was coming to spend the
night, and even on those nights the
Jefferson Rose quilt was removed from the
bed at bedtime and replaced with a plain
quilt.

[6] Detail of number 5.

[7] Home of Barbara Ford.

[8] Barbara Ford, quiltmaker.

Quilts such as these were highly prized. One is mentioned in a will recorded at the Jonesborough courthouse by Jacob Miller, Sr., a son of early settlers. Jacob married Elizabeth Range in 1798, and she made the Rose quilt sometime before her death in 1843. The will, which was signed and dated in 1857, reads in part:

> To my grand daughter who now lives with me, Mary Devault, I give and bequeath my SideBoard, Desk, One half of my kitchen Furniture or kitchen utensils, one feather and one straw bed, bedstead, and well furnished with suitable bedclothing for same, also my quilted quilt of the pattern known and called 'Rose of Sharon'. . . .

By 1830, in little more than fifty years, substantial communities had grown out of the wilderness. Primitive cabins were replaced with houses of planed lumber, brick, or stone; and interiors were furnished for a more comfortable life. There was time to make fancy quilts for bridal beds and company.

It is rare to find utility quilts surviving from the late eighteenth and early nineteenth centuries simply because they were used up. When they were no longer suitable for bedcovers or for recovering with a new top, there were other uses: padding against bedsprings or on a wagon-bottom, stuffing for insulation, or covering for produce, goods, or implements. A quilt can have many lives; it is not disposed of lightly. The majority of quilts that do remain are the "best" quilts, which were saved for special occasions and treated with great respect.

Our survey recorded seven quilts that were thought to have been made before 1840 and brought into the state soon thereafter. Three of these are of the broderie perse style, which is of English derivation. Chintz and finely printed cottons were used for applique and for piecing with plain linen or cotton background material. These three quilts came from Virginia and South Carolina where a number of outstanding examples presently remain.[4]

The other four are varied. One is a pieced quilt, Tulip in a Basket, from the Lane family of Fairfax, Virginia. Made earlier, it was brought to McMinnville, Tennessee, in 1846 by Alfred Sidney Lane and his new wife, Emily F. Garretson. Its large size shows that it was made for a high bed, perhaps one which required steps beside it for access. The second quilt is a friendship quilt made by the Ladies' Society of the Lutheran Church of Baltimore, Maryland. According to family tradition, it was given to the Reverend William Jenkins who left Baltimore for Tennessee in 1824 to establish three Lutheran churches in the Shelbyville area. The quilt is typical of the Baltimore album quilts that were produced in mid-century.[5]

The last two of the early quilts were given to the Memphis Pink Palace Museum some years ago; both have no accompanying information. They are a pair of woolen wholecloth quilts, one of indigo blue and one of saffron yellow, stuffed with wool and backed with woolen cloth. Their medallion and border quilting designs are identical. Quilts of this type—spanning the period from 1730 to 1830—may be seen in historic homes and museums in the Northeast.[6] Their origin will doubtless remain a mystery.

It is evident from the survey that the period preceding the Civil War was a time for extraordinary quiltmaking. Considering how many quilts were donated to the Confederate cause, it is fortunate that so many remain.[7] Antebellum quiltmakers were expected to practice their quiltmaking and needlework as essential preparation for marriage, which also included knowledge of butchering, gardening, weaving, animal husbandry, crop production, and the usual cooking and laundry. In addition to being skilled at sewing, a quiltmaker had to grow and prepare cotton for filler before she could make a quilt.

Throughout the survey we saw quilts made from homegrown materials. Nineteenth-century Tennessee was an agrarian state, with many families maintaining an almost self-sufficient existence. This practice was carried on well into the twentieth century, and some quilters remember carding cotton for filler or seeing their mothers card. Others had grandparents who grew cotton, made hand-carded batts, spun thread, and wove and dyed cloth. They depended very little on commercial products, which were difficult to obtain in the lean years. Even after ready-made batting was available, many households continued to use their own cotton and wool out of habit and economy.

In examining quilts during the survey, it was sometimes possible for us to distinguish handspun, handwoven backing material, especially if a quilt came from a family of weavers. More often, we could not tell for certain. According to Doris Kennedy and Sadye Tune Wilson, authors of *Of Coverlets*, even the experts cannot tell by a cursory examination.[8] It was observed that handwoven lengths of backing were more likely to have seams with butting edges, rather than inside seams.

## [9] WHIG ROSE.

*Maker:* Mother of Hester Gregg Susong. Greene County, circa 1835-1850.
*Lender:* Kathryn Susong Neas, great-great-granddaughter.
*Pieced:* 87½″ x 68″; cotton: red and green solids with green, red, pink and brown prints; white background; white handwoven and handspun cotton back; binding of green print fabric on the straight; quilting by the piece in the blocks, quilted and stuffed garlands cross the surface lengthwise, rows of clam-shell quilting in the background, and running vine in the borders; flower buds are appliqued, embroidered stamens added.

The quilt was one of many in the survey said to have been buried during the War Between the States so that it would not be taken by soldiers, who were badly in need of warm blankets and quilts. Usually floral patterns of the nineteenth century were appliqued; but this one is pieced, as were several others found during the survey. Although many stuffed quilts were found in Rhea County in Lower East Tennessee, this is one of several found in Greene County, in Upper East Tennessee.

For detail see page 45.

11

[**10**] SAMPLER OF BLOCKS.

*Maker:* Iora Almina Philo Pool.
   Sunbright, Morgan County, circa 1870.
*Owners:* Betty Holman Pickett and Gwen
   Holman Kelly, great-granddaughters.
*Pieced:* 83″ x 75½″; cotton: assorted
   fabrics, predominately brown; unfinished
   top.

Dozens of traditional and original blocks in
small and miniature scale are evidence of
the maker's desire to make as many
different blocks as she could. Having no
regular set, the units flow into each other
in happy medley.

For detail see page 108.

Tennessee was a politically divided state during the Civil War and had many strong Union supporters, especially in the eastern part of the state. Even so, it suffered the same economic depression as the rest of the South. Resources—material, spiritual, and human—were greatly depleted. Recovery was long and slow. In the quilts made during this time it is possible to see the sacrifice, making-do, and poverty of the postwar period. Scrap quilts were made by necessity. They are numerous, and their character is distinct.

Jeannette Lasansky has noted the difference between the scrap quilts of Pennsylvania and Tennessee. Patterns are similar or identical, as would be expected with the population exchange between the two states; but the difference is that cloth was easily obtained at a reasonable price in Pennsylvania. Quiltmakers there were able to purchase material just for the making of quilts, and any leftover fabric went into the making of scrap quilts. In contrast, the utility and scrap-made quilts of Tennessee often look quite different since they were made from the frugal saving of every available household scrap.[9] The habit has been retained by some regional quiltmakers who rely entirely on their scrapbag collections of cloth for quiltmaking. They still believe that purchased material is only for the making of a "company" quilt.[10]

It is not apparent from the sampling of 1425 quilts documented during the survey that one type or pattern is typical of Tennessee quilts. Michael Kile says he thinks of the dark tones of everyday pieced quilts and the pattern known as New York Beauty when he thinks of this state.[11] Others are impressed with the fine applique and stuffed work of the mid-nineteenth century. We can see how accurate these impressions are when we study the profile of the survey.

Here is a listing of the categories:

[11] Detail of number 1, page vi.

| Pieced | 1,050 |
|---|---|
| Appliqued | 199 |
| Crazy-patch | 78 |
| Combination | 59 |
| Wholecloth | 20 |
| Embroidered | 11 |
| Novelty | 8 |
| | 1,425 |

13

[**12**] Emmett A. Roper, Sr. at the age of 27. Photo taken October 4, 1888. See number 1 on page vi.

Forty-seven of the pieced quilts are in the string-quilt technique. Combination quilts are those combining nearly equal amounts of piecing and applique. Novelties include Yo-Yo and Puff quilts. Embroidered quilts are those whose major motifs are stitched and do not include embellishment, as in Crazy quilts.

Close to two-thirds of the 1,425 quilts were pieced. Star patterns of great variety were the most abundant designs, with a total of 164. They came in every color, shape, and size, and under the many following names: Arrowhead Star, Blazing Star, Broken Star, Circle of Stars, Crescent and Star, Dolly Madison, Eight-pointed Star, Feathered Star, Fence Row Star, Four-pointed Star, Glitter Star, Harlequin Star, Harvest Sun, Hex Star, Iowa Star, King's Star, Lone Star, The Lost Sheep, Mexican Star, Ohio Star, Old-Fashioned Star, Pierre, Radiant Star [Plate 00], Rolling Star, Sawtooth Star, Seven Sisters, Six-Pointed Star, Spider Web, Star and Diamond, Star Bouquet, Star of Bethlehem, Star of Destiny, Star of the East, Star of LeMoyne, Texas Star, Variable Star, and Virginia.

[**13**] R A D I A N T  S T A R.

*Maker:* Mary Elizabeth Waggoner
  Moorehead.
  Moore County, circa 1890.
*Lender:* Evelyn Grant Knight,
  great-granddaughter.
*Pieced:* 85¼″ x 71¼″; cotton: red, brown,
  navy, white; white gauze-like back; green
  binding (faded); quilted in parallel rows
  ½″ apart.

Mary Elizabeth grew up in a family of ten
children. After marrying John Moorehead,
they had a family of nine children. Her
quilt signifies her character and
personality. She was a well-organized
woman who found time for the pleasures of
quilting. Her photograph shows the
graceful hands of an accomplished
craftsman and her choice of color and
diagonal-block arrangement confirm it.

15

[**14**] Detail of number 13.

The most-used patterns, in order of frequency, were the Lone Star or Star of Bethlehem, Star of LeMoyne, Seven Sisters, Harvest Sun, Feathered Star, Blazing Star, and Broken Star. Several reasons can be given for the star's popularity as a quilt pattern. Many of the designs are suitable for scrap-piecing and can become extremely handsome when augmented with good quilting. Some of the patterns are relatively easy to piece and offer pleasant work for relaxation. Almost every star block has a visually satisfying quality that is arrived at by a balance of proportion, rhythm, and variety of relationship. Then, too, the religious connotation of the Star of Bethlehem is significant to quiltmakers of the Christian faith.

[15] Quiltmaker, Mary Elizabeth Waggoner Moorehead, maker of the Radient Star, and her two daughters.

17

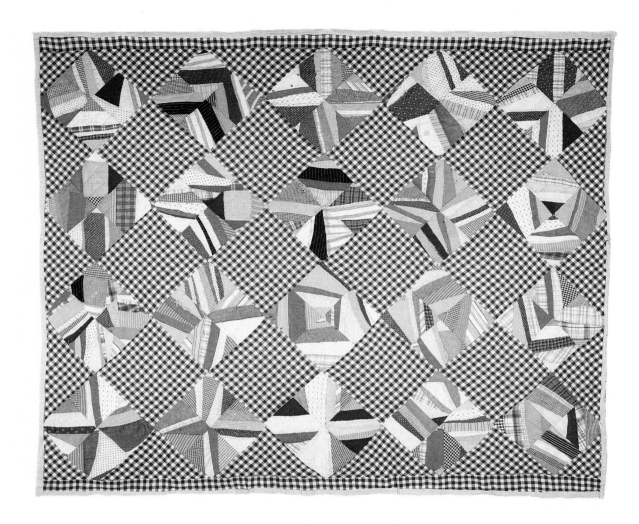

**[16]** STRING.

*Maker:* Florence Ellen LaFollette.
  Pigeon Forge, Sevier County, 1920.
*Lender:* Polly LaFollette, daughter-in-law.
*Pieced in the string method:* 70½" x 59½";
  cotton: assorted blue calicos in the blocks
  and a black-and-white check fabric in the
  plain blocks; yellow muslin back; edge
  has back turned to front; batting is a
  white woven coverlet; quilting is in
  groups of three parallel diagonal lines all
  over the surface of the quilt.

Florence LaFollette pieced and quilted this
quilt. It was given as a wedding gift in
1929 to the current owner, whose husband
is the son of the maker. The string method,
using scrap fabrics, is a common type of
quilt in Tennessee. This one has a striking
optical design overall.

18

**[17] BLUE PATCHWORK CROSS**
(Unequal Nine Patch).

*Maker:* Pamona Louvicy Forester Stuart
   (Monie); quilter: Bertha May Stuart
   Boulton.
   Sugar Creek, Hickman County.
   1895 or 96, quilted circa 1930.
*Lender:* Martha Boulton Shelton,
   granddaughter and daughter.
*String-pieced:* 80½" x 74¾"; cotton: pink,
   navy, green, light blue, black, white;
   floral print back; front edge turned to
   back on two sides, back to front on two
   sides; allover shell quilting with black
   thread.

Pamona pieced the Blue Patchwork Cross
early in her marriage and laid it aside to
help her husband build a handsome
two-story house, then rear two daughters.
Bertha May, the younger, married at
seventeen against the wishes of her parents,
who wanted her to attend college. She
"took hold" as a farmer's wife who could
assist with the numerous chores, rear five
children, and quilt. Her mother's quilt
served her family well.

Forty-seven of the pieced quilts were made with the string-piecing
method. String quilts are made of irregular strips and scraps stitched
together to form a unit for piecing. They are intended for everyday
use and are not always put together with great care. String quilts make
use of narrow strips and pieces too small for regular quilt pieces. The
usual practice is to sew strips together by seaming them onto a cut-
newspaper, or cloth, pattern. Overhanging ends are trimmed and the
paper is removed. The units are joined together or put with plain
blocks (See illustration no. 16) or sashing to form a quilt top. Snowball, Kite, Spider Web, Rocky Road to Kansas, Star of LeMoyne, and
One Patch squares are popular patterns for string quilts. These quilts
are usually regarded as the lowliest of quilts made from the meagerest
of scraps, yet the irregularity of pieces and coloration can sometimes
result in a visually strong work from the hand of an untutored quiltmaker.[12]

[**18**] Detail of number 17.

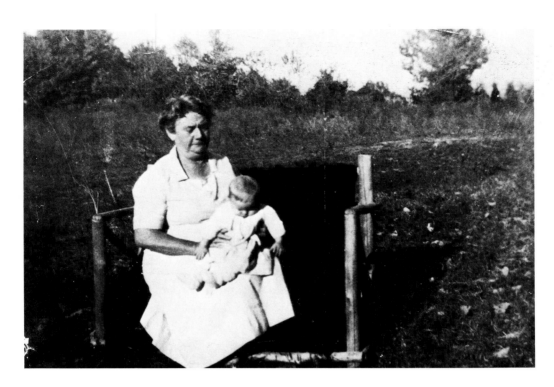

[19] Quiltmaker, Pamona Louvicy Forester Stuart, with her granddaughter, Margaret Ann Boulton, in 1935.

[20] Home of Milton and Pamona Stuart on Sugar Creek in Middle Tennessee in May 1974. Porch railing on lower porch rotted away years earlier.

**[21] BASKET QUILT** (Confederate Fund-Raiser).

*Maker:* Mary High Prince and friends.
 Raus Community, Bedford County,
 1863-64.
*Owner:* Emeline Prince Gist.
*Pieced:* 96″ x 74″; cotton and linen:
 assorted scraps; muslin back; grey bias
 edge, perhaps added later; quilted by the
 piece with background in one-inch
 squares.

Each block has the name of the maker or a
Tennessee Volunteer written in pokeberry
ink. Two poems are also inscribed. When
she was seventy, in 1910, Mary pieced a
pillow of scraps from homespun dresses she
and her friends had worn during the War
Between the States. On the pillow she
stitched these lines:

Hoorah! for the home spun
dresses we southern ladies
wore in time of the war.
Ev'ry piece here.
Sad memories it brings
back to me.
For our hearts was weary
and restless.
And our life was full of care.
The burden laid up on us
seemed greater than
we could bear.

22

Baskets have long been favorites with many quilters. This was borne out in the documentation of thirty-five basket quilts in several different pieced patterns. One of the oldest basket quilts we saw in the survey, made before 1840, has already been mentioned. Made in Fairfax, Virginia, it has generous proportions and the orderly grace of a quilt made in a home acquainted with refinement.

One Cherry Basket quilt was made in 1863 and 1864 as a fund raiser for Confederate forces (See illustration no. 21). It was one of several raffled by the ladies of the Raus community in Bedford County. Makers' names are inscribed in ink, as well as names of several Tennessee Volunteers serving in the 17th Tennessee Infantry Regiment. This basket quilt and another became the property of Mary High Prince, one of the makers, who later said the quilt was hidden in stumps for safekeeping during Yankee looting raids in the area. Mary herself was involved in a tale of daring adventure and grief. She was a Confederate spy who was once caught while carrying a message to forces in Columbia, Tennessee. She was able to back up to the fire and destroy the message before it was found. Since there was no evidence, she was let go. Her fiancé, also a Confederate spy, was caught and hanged in Murfreesboro. Enlisting the aid of his sister, she drove a wagon to Murfreesboro, cut down the body, and brought it back to Raus for burial. The rather tame, quietly composed Basket quilt gives no hint of the personality of its plucky owner who lived to be 91. Mary's granddaughter, Emeline Prince Gist, inherited the quilt from her father, Mary's son.

Like the star patterns, basket quilts are attractive when made from assorted scraps. The change of color and tone in the fabric enlivens the surface and brings variety. Baskets are satisfying and complete units which perhaps may hold hidden thoughts for their makers. Baskets can have many meanings: gathering, hiding, collecting, organizing, giving, making, or possessing. Baskets have universal appeal.

*Great-great-grandmother Polly Ann Kinkead loaned her Feathered Star quilt to a Confederate soldier when he hid in a cave behind the house to escape capture. It wasn't found until some years later, reminding the maker of her part in history.*
—Maryana S. Huff

23

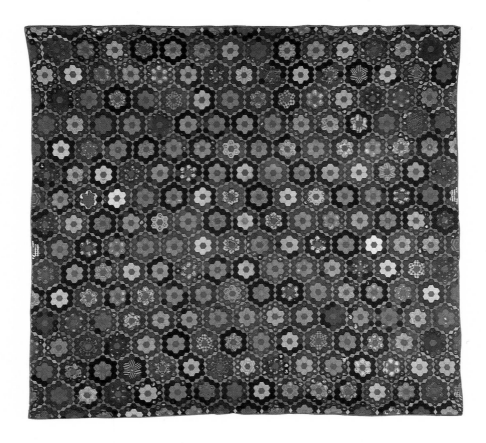

**[22] MARTHA WASHINGTON'S FLOWER GARDEN.**

*Maker:* Eliza Benton Boyles Bagley.
  Fayetteville, Lincoln County, 1860.
*Lender:* Ellen Goodrich Morgan,
  great-granddaughter.
*Pieced:* 90¾" x 85"; wool: dark assorted
  colors set with lavender; home-dyed
  brown cotton back; woven wool braid at
  edge; quilted by the piece in black
  thread.

Mrs. Bagley pieced her quilt by the English template method and used 217 whole blocks and forty-five half blocks set together with very small diamonds. She undertook her ambitious project with usual determination at the age of forty-five. Eliza Bagley was noted for her fine needlework in embroidery and quiltmaking. Her strong character was exemplified when she rode horseback from Fayetteville to Chickamauga, Georgia, to move her son, injured in the War Between the States, to her sister's home in Alabama for recovery.

  The mosaic hexagon was, and still is, a popular English quilt pattern. Undoubtedly its American zenith was reached in the 1930s and 1940s.

[**23**] Detail of number 22.

[**24**] Quiltmaker, Eliza Benton Boyles
Bagley.

25

[25] WORSTED QUILT (Dresden Plate).

*Maker:* Martha Elizabeth Brooks Randolph. Lincoln County, circa 1890.
*Lender:* Mildred Elizabeth Rawls Stovall, great-granddaughter.
*Pieced and appliqued:* 80½″ x 69″; wool: assorted red, blue and white; unlined, assorted block foundation material; blue and white striped binding; unquilted.

Mrs. Randolph used what she had for her center blocks and made a charming composition with the unmatched units. The crazy-pieced border adds yet another trace of humor. She was a brave woman who at twenty-one years of age married a widower with eleven children, and they had four more of their own. She made all their clothes, socks, quilts, and blankets and attended to chores of a farm.

[26] Quiltmaker, Martha Elizabeth Brooks Randolph, at work on her farm in Middle Tennessee.

Close to the baskets in number, and also suitable for scrap-piecing, were the Double Wedding Ring (36), Grandmother's Flower Garden (29), hexagon mosaics in various arrangements (19), and the Dresden Plate (25). The last named is pieced and then applied to the background material. Some of these quilts may have been made after the survey's cut-off date of 1930, as some owners were uncertain of the exact date of origin.

[27] LOG CABIN IN SQUARES
AND DIAMONDS.

*Maker:* a member of McGill, Hix, Reagor,
    or Gardner family.
    Bedford County, circa 1870.
*Lender:* Sarah Thomas, descendant.
*Pieced:* 95³/₄″ x 77¹/₄″; wool: red, blue, and
    black; unlined, foundation material
    assorted cotton prints and muslin;
    unbound; unquilted.

Sarah Thomas was reared in the home of
her maternal grandparents, and from
several branches of her family she inherited
quilts whose makers are unidentified. It
took 238 blocks to make the top. The set of
the blocks is an unusual arrangement of the
Log Cabin lights and shadows.

28

[28] Detail of number 27.

Several simple, straightforward designs have proven themselves worthy of frequent repetition over a long period of time. They are the Log Cabin (25 in our survey), Nine Patch (22), Rocky Mountain (23), Double Irish Chain (20), Triple Irish Chain (18), Trip Around the World (17), Pine Tree (17), Grandmother's Fan (16), and Ocean Waves (16). The exception in this group of simple patterns is the Rocky Mountain pattern, also known as New York Beauty (See illustrations no. 29 and 30). Crown of Thorns, Life Everlasting, and Sunset are other names used in Tennessee. This is not an easy quilt to make. The cutting must be accurate and the piecing exact or the points will not be true. It was surprising to find twenty-three of these quilts, considering the intricacy of the work. The quiltmakers were not equally successful in their efforts, and some produced quilts with mismatched points and irregularities. Two of the documented quilts are thought to have been made in the 1840s, and one is included from beyond our survey period, 1945. At least one example was made in every decade except the 1910s, twelve of them between 1850 and 1880.

*"I can remember watching Mother and Grandmother piece this quilt. They used scraps left from their dresses and the pieces all mean something to me."*
—Elizabeth Cunningham about a Dresden Plate quilt

29

**[29] CROWN OF THORNS** (New York Beauty).

*Maker:* Mrs. D. P. Walker.
 Sweetwater Valley, Monroe County, circa 1840.
*Lender:* Carolyn Hodge Rogers,
 great-great-granddaughter.
*Pieced:* 87¼" x 74¾"; cotton: solid red, blue resist-dot, white; white back, possibly handwoven; blue resist-dot binding on the straight; quilted vines, garlands, circular motifs.

It is thought that this quilt was made by Mrs. Walker for her daughter's wedding, which occurred about 1840. Twenty-three quilts of this pattern were found during the survey, and this is the finest of them all. The delicacy of the quilting designs are more akin to lacemaking than to quiltmaking. The diagonal set of the blocks and strips is more dramatic than is a horizontal and vertical setting.

[30] Quiltmaker and husband, Mr. and Mrs. D. P. Walker of Sweetwater Valley.

[31] Full view of number 29.

[**32**] Detail of number 34.

[**33**] Quiltmaker, Annie B. Anderson of Knoxville.

Laurel Horton has made the comment that during the South Carolina quilt survey she found an unexpected number of Rocky Mountain quilts in the upland region of the state. Some of them were poorly executed, as if they might have been a training project for novice quiltmakers. If so, some of the students received poor marks, in her judgment.[13]

Other pieced quilt patterns—Churn Dash and Monkey Wrench, One Patch, Drunkard's Path, Peony, Brickwork, Snowball, and Triangles—were seen ten to twelve times. Forty other pieced patterns were recorded twice. There were 115 named patterns that appeared only once, and scattered numbers of patterns were seen between two and ten times. We were unable to name and identify fourteen quilt patterns. Some others were named by their owners or makers but are not found in Barbara Brackman's *An Encyclopedia of Pieced Quilt Patterns*, or other reference books. Undoubtedly, some may have been quilts of original design, but they were seemingly few. The untutored kind of art called "folk art" was seldom encountered in the survey.

## [34] BRICK.

*Maker:* Annie Burnett Anderson.
  Knoxville, Knox County, circa 1900.
*Lender:* Terry Irwin, great-grandson.
*Pieced:* 69¼" x 68¾"; wool: black, tan
  and brown; gray chambray back; batting
  is a handwoven wool blanket; edge has
  back turned to front; quilting is in
  diagonal rows three inches apart
  extending all over the surface of the
  quilt; special surface techniques include
  embroidery over seams.

The quilt has embroidery techniques
similar to Victorian crazy quilts that were
being made in the late 1800s and early
1900s, and it is representative of brick
quilts made with samples of men's wool
suiting fabric. However, this quilt is like
none other seen in the survey. The
quiltmaker consciously or unconsciously
used the simple brick pattern in a creative
way to make a memorable masterpiece.

33

*"Our earliest dresses are in this quilt. It was pieced on shares, with the maker returning half the blocks and keeping half for herself."*
—Ann Chittenden

The variety of the 1,050 pieced quilts, their patterns, and the range of proficiency of the quiltmakers give a sampling of the economic and social status of Tennessee households in a span of 130 years. Quilts made out of men's old pants legs indicate the need for warmth in a low-income family. Old quilts covered by newer tops show frugality of time and material. Well-made quilts of all-new material, filled with home-grown cotton, show the work of many women preparing for marriage. The silk pieced-basket quilt belonging to President Andrew Johnson's granddaughter speaks of the 1920s and luxury.

Crazy quilts made another large group of quilts; they are distantly related to string quilts. They were found in all parts of the state and were made during the fad which swept the nation from 1876 to 1900. Their survival and abundance (there were seventy-eight in the survey) can partially be attributed to their impracticality since the more elegant of these quilts, or throws, were made as works of needleart, rather than as useful bedcovers. The fancy-work examples were found primarily in the larger cities, where rich fabrics and trimmings were available. Many seem to have been made from the dressmaking scraps of relatives and friends. Other fabrics may have come from the kits and mail order assortments described by Penny McMorris in *Crazy Quilts*.[14]

34

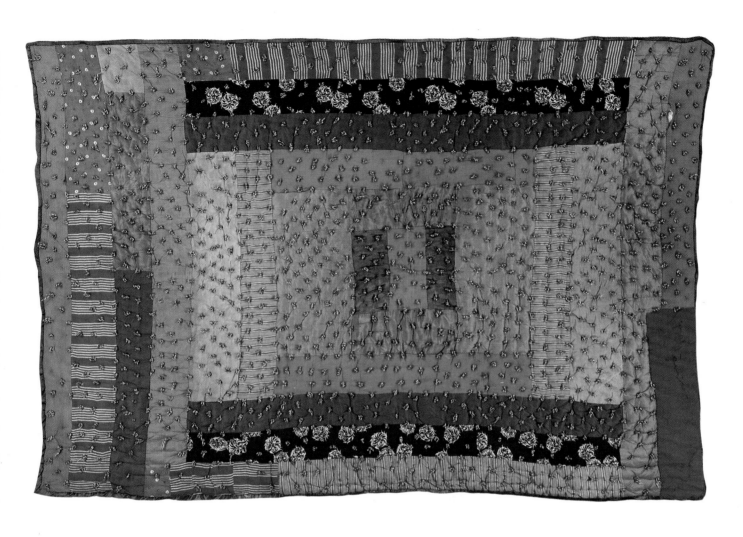

**[35] LOG CABIN** (Pig Pen).

*Maker:* Blanche Hurst Pangle.
　Knoxville, Knox County, circa 1910.
*Lender:* Judy Pratt.
*Pieced:* 82″ x 58″; silk: muted tones of
　navy, green, orange, and rose; some
　printed fabric; purple cotton back;
　binding of purple silk; wool batting; tied
　with white and black wool yarn.

Blanche Hurst Pangle used to make up the
patterns for her quilts. Her daughter
remembers her mother going to the mill
area on Jackson Avenue in Knoxville to buy
uncarded wool for her quiltmaking. This is
an innovative use of a common pattern
(Log Cabin) with unusual fabrics (silk) and
colors. The density of the wool batt caused
the quiltmaker to tie rather than quilt.

35

**[36] CRAZY QUILT.**

*Maker:* Amy Terrass Johnson.
 Chattanooga, Hamilton County, 1883.
*Lender:* Tennessee State Museum, gift of
 Dr. and Mrs. Robert Haley, Jr.
*Crazy-patch:* 73″ x 71″; silk- and
 cotton-velvet: assorted deep, rich colors;
 maroon velvet border; gold silk back;
 gold silk cord set between top and
 bottom knife-edge; blind-tacked; heavily
 embroidered, with painting,
 ribbon-work, a photograph, a stuffed
 strawberry, and 16 three-dimensional
 dolls.

This magnificent crazy quilt was an
ambitious project for its maker. The
numerous dolls and animals were surely
intended for childhood delight. The
separately-made dolls are most unusual.

36

[37] Detail views of number 36.

One gathered scraps where one could.[15] Viola Rudder, for example, worked as a milliner in a Knoxville department store about 1905, and she brought home silk- and cotton-velvet scraps for quiltmaking. Her mother and sister, Florence and Frances Rudder, used them to make a crazy quilt. The pieces in the 10-inch blocks are fairly large and mostly rectangular, giving a bold image in an organized format. The pieces and blocks are outlined in a simple featherstitch.

Earlier crazy quilts, even though made on a rectangular cloth base, show less block definition. Scraps were intentionally angular and asymmetrical to achieve the "crazed" look. Fashion dictated the working of an abundance of elaborate stitches in silk, wool, or cotton thread. Young ladies attended needlework classes to learn the latest stitches and honed their skills on the blocks of a crazy quilt.

Crazy quilts seem to be accompanied by stories more often than do other types of quilts. Betty Tharp was a girl who had finished her masterpiece quilt of rich scraps and fancy stitches by the time she was eighteen. For the next two years she attended Brownsville College in West Tennessee, where she was an eager student and the editor of the school newspaper. She died at the age of twenty from consumption, it is said, and a cold caught from late-hour studying. Her wonderful quilt of silks and velvets, set off with a luxurious blue velvet border, became the property of Betty's sister, Florence Tharp Edenton. Passed down in the family, it now belongs to Betty's great-great-niece, Carolyn Gilley Maples.

# BOOK CORNER

410 Meeting St.
West Columbia
794-6200

Cynthia Manning
Bookseller

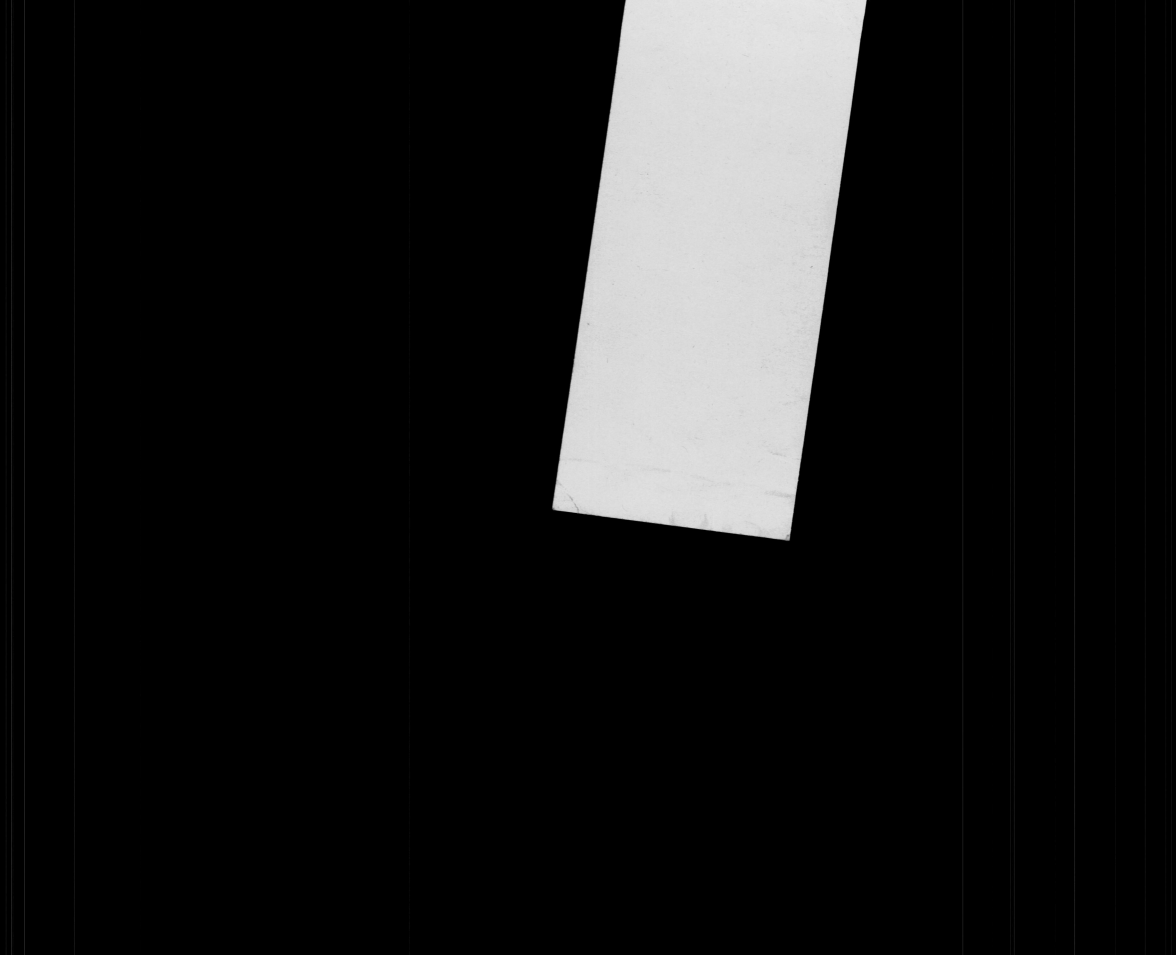

## [38] SOULE COLLEGE QUILT

*Maker:* Classmates at Soule College.
  Murfreesboro, Rutherford County, 1891.
*Lender:* Jeanne Gilmore Webb.
*Pieced:* 74″ x 71½″; wool and velvet:
  assorted colors; back is red cotton;
  binding is tan woven braid; no batting;
  quilt is tacked at corners of blocks;
  embroidery of names, floral motifs, and
  overlapping edges is in various fancy
  stitches using wool thread and some
  pearl cotton thread.

Quilt was made by classmates at Soule
College of Murfreesboro as a gift to J. N.
Holt, an itinerant Cumberland Presbyterian
preacher in the Rutherford County area.
Many Victorian crazy quilts of Middle
Tennessee differ from other Victorian crazy
quilts in that they are made of wool rather
than silk.

[**39**] Full view of number 38.

A plaque in Murfreesboro identifies the site of Soule College, which included needlework in its curriculum. When Jeanne Webb brought a quilt that had been made at the school, we asked her to tell about it (See illustrations no. 38 and 39).

"Soule College, a long-lived and prestigious private boarding school for girls located in Murfreesboro, Tennessee, opened for classes in the old Female Academy in September 1851 and closed finally in May 1917 after public schools had gained popularity.[16] Named for Methodist Bishop Joshua Soule, the school maintained high academic standards throughout its existence, offering languages, science, mathematics, humanities, music, art, and needlework. Although affiliated with the Methodist church, the school accepted girls from other religious denominations.

"In 1891 students at the school made a presentation quilt for J. N. Holt, an itinerant Cumberland Presbyterian minister for

[**40**] Detail of number 39.

Rutherford County and vicinity. The quilt has twenty-five blocks with embroidered names of the makers, the date '1891' (five times), 'J. N. Holt' and 'S. L. S.,' the initials of Reverend Holt's wife, Susan L. Smotherman. Fabrics used are mostly lightweight wool with a few velvets and silks. Most of the embroidery is done in crewel yarn. The elaborate floral designs and symbols are characteristic of the time, as is fancy stitching over the seams. The embroidered surnames on the quilt—Tune, Steele, Green, Parsons, Knott, Burton, Landers, and Vanetta—are still familiar names in Middle Tennessee."

Reverend Holt gave the quilt to his nephew, J. N. Smotherman, and his wife Mary, with whom he resided in late years. In turn, Mary went to live with her niece, Jeanne Gilmore Webb, the present owner of the Soule College wool crazy quilt.

**[41]** ROSE OF SHARON.

*Maker:* Possibly the Rowden Sisters. Meigs County, circa 1880.

*Lender:* Mrs. W. A. Shadow. (Since the survey was taken, the quilt has been donated to the McMinn County Living Heritage Museum by Mrs. Shadow and her daughter, Muriel S. Mayfield.)

*Applique:* 95″ x 87″; cotton: yellow-green, red, and rose prints, yellow solid, white background; white back; rose calico bias edge; quilted floral design identical to applique motif.

When Mrs. Shadow was nursing a member of the Rowden family in 1935, she noticed a cigarette hole the brother had burned in the quilt. She commented that it was a beautiful quilt and offered to take it home for mending. The sisters insisted she keep the quilt as a token of their appreciation for her kind service to their brother. The simple border serves as an adequate frame to contain the blocks.

[**42**] Detail of number 41.

These wool crazy quilts, which comprised a third of the crazy quilt grouping, are derived from the silk-and-velvet high fashion tradition. They have less conformity, more ingenuity, and a certain naive charm. The texture and color of the wool give a pleasing surface quality that invites the touch. Unlike the silk and velvet quilts, there is a comfortable homeliness to them. This type predominates in Middle Tennessee.

Billy Marlin's great-great-aunt, Mary Ellen Tomerlin, made a crazy quilt of wool, signed "June 11, 1891," on which she stitched dozens of wonderful items. A visit to Grandmother's house meant a chance to see Mary Ellen's quilt and look for the embroidered snake, elephant, tiger, kitten in a boat, shooting star, rabbit, pod of peas, dragonfly, grouse, sun, moon, frog, and all manner of flowers and insects. There was so much to see, the objects defied counting. It was fine entertainment.

[44] Full view of number 43.

## [43] ROSE TREE.

*Maker:* Annie Price and Laura Little. Shady Valley, Johnson County, circa 1861 appliqued; 1884 quilted.
*Lender:* Lorene Little Mantooth
*Applique:* 75″ x 71″; cotton: green, yellow-orange, green calico print; white background; white handwoven back; white with floral-print binding on the straight; quilting is diamond quilting in the plain blocks, a leaf garland in the sashing and stipple contour quilting in background of the applique blocks.

Annie Price made the quilt top in 1861, and gave it to her sister, Mrs. Sampson Cole, whose daughter, Mrs. James Madison Little, quilted it in 1884. The quilt is more innovative than most applique quilts. The leaves are stylized, as are the baskets. The sashing includes small dots appliqued on the quilted garlands. The diagonal arrangement of the blocks produces a strong visual image. The quilt belongs to the family of Laura Little's great-grandson.

And finally in the survey we found a few crazy quilts made of cotton. While the pieces are irregular and sometimes embroidered, they are quite different from their wool and silk cousins. Their essence seems to be utility rather than glamor or elegance; they were more closely related to practical string quilts.

In addition to the 1,050 pieced quilts in the survey of 1,425 quilts, 199 were applique and fifty-nine were a combination of applique and piecing. It is apparent that more quilters preferred to make pieced quilts, or perhaps chose to make them because they required less expenditure. The percentage of applique quilts in the study is probably higher than the actual percentage produced. Since most applique quilts were made for occasional use, their preservation has been greater than that of everyday quilts. Then, too, present-day owners tended to bring their best, most historic quilts for documentation.

Over half the quilts in the applique group have flowers and leaves for their subject, sometimes in combination with vases or urns. The rose appeared sixty-four times in many forms: Whig Rose, Rose of Sharon, Jefferson Rose, Virginia Rose, Colonial Rose, Ohio Rose, and Rose Tree. Its symbolism stands for love, simplicity, purity, beauty, and bliss.[17] The Rose of Sharon pattern reflects the Biblical poetry of the Song of Solomon, a favorite book read by young ladies of the nineteenth century.

Twelve examples of a Rose of Sharon block with four or more buds, *totally pieced*, were recorded in the survey. They were made in the mid-nineteenth century and are not generally recognized as being pieced, due to the familiarity of the appliqued rose.[18] Florence Peto, in *American Quilts and Coverlets*, points out a pieced rose that is appliqued to the background, unlike these which have the background pieced into the rose.[19]

[45] Detail of number 9, page 11.

*"Aunt Argie Stem collected scraps for her Double Wedding Ring quilt from students at the Rover one-room school. Everyone had a part in her quilt."*
—Barbara Crockett Troxler

45

**[46]** COCKSCOMB & CURRANTS.

*Maker:* Jane Richey Morelock.
  Cleveland, Bradley County, circa 1870.
*Lender:* Mary K. Morelock Ledford,
  granddaughter.
*Applique:* 79″ and 64½″; cotton: red,
  yellow-orange, green calico print; white
  background; white cotton muslin back;
  pink binding on the straight; quilting
  ¾″ diamond in background and
  following the pattern of the applique in
  the blocks; some of the applique is by
  machine.

Born in 1818 in Blount County, Jane
Richey Morelock made several quilts, this
one in Bradley County after her marriage in
1833. Cockscomb & Currants appeared
twelve times in the survey. This one
represents an early division of the overall
space—four quadrants with no border.

46

[47] Quiltmaker, Jane Richey Morelock of Bradley County.

The majority of applique quilts were found in East Tennessee, some in Middle Tennessee, and fewer in West Tennessee. The Tulip (16), Cockscomb and Currant (12), and Princess Feather (17) quilts seen were almost always splendid examples of applique work and quilting. They were made for special reasons at considerable expense. The quilts made before the Civil War usually have large units of work, with some as few as four blocks making a top. As the century progressed, blocks were reduced in size; and by the 1920s some were down to ten inches and required many to make a top.

There were twenty-two doll quilts: Overall Boy, Sunbonnet Baby, and other variations. Some may have been made after 1930, but they were included because of uncertainty of date by the owners. Various single designs account for the remainder of the applique quilts. Of course, most applique quilts do have a certain amount of piecing when the blocks and sets are assembled and joined. A number of quilts combine pieced work and applique in more or less even amounts. These include among others: Dresden Plate, Chestnut Bud, Oak Leaf and Reel, and some friendship quilts.[20]

In addition, there were twenty wholecloth quilts and eight novelty quilts: Yo-Yo (4), Puff (2), Cocklebur (1), and one crayon-drawn. Eleven quilts had embroidered designs as the basic motifs.

47

**[48] BIBLE VERSES QUILT.**

*Maker:* Jemima Patton Clark.
   Christiana, Rutherford County, circa
   1922.
*Lender:* Charlotte Haymore Clark,
   granddaughter-in-law.
*Pieced and embroidered:* 85½" x 74½";
   cotton: blue and white solid; red and
   white cotton embroidery thread; blue
   and white print back; blue bias binding;
   allover 1" rows of quilting.

Mrs. Clark made this quilt as a fund-raiser
for her church missionary society. She
charged a certain amount, perhaps $.25,
for each donor's favorite Bible verse to be
embroidered on a block. Her small
grandson, William F. Clark, II, was sent
on frequent trips to the store with his pony
to buy more Turkey red embroidery thread.

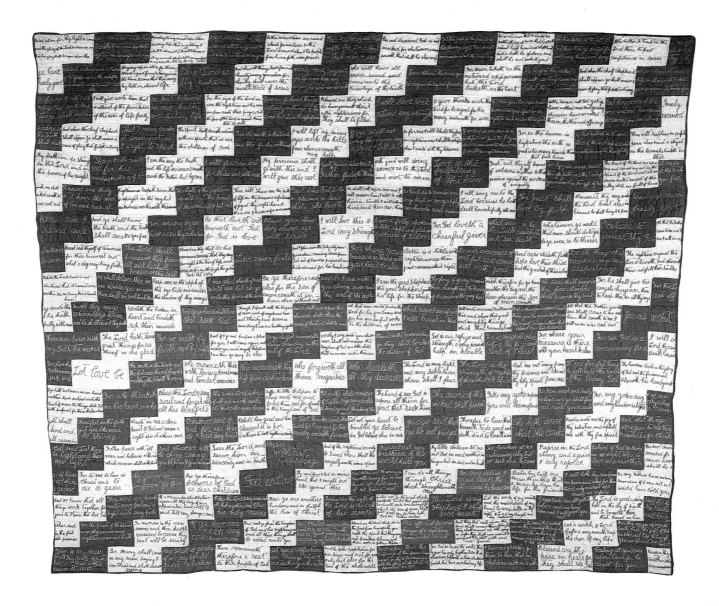

[**49**] Full view of number 48.

49

[**50**] TREE OF LIFE.

*Maker:* Mother of Miss Sally Bohannon.
  Greeneville, Greene County, circa 1850.
*Owner:* Lucille Bohannon Thomas,
  great-niece.
*Pieced and applique:* 90½" x 76"; cotton:
  red, pink, orange, green, and white
  solids; white back, possibly linen; red
  binding; double-row quilting by the
  piece in red, green, and white thread.

The Tree of Life has been called a symbol
of immortality by some. The luscious fruit
of the tree shown here seems to be more
closely related to the tempting fruit of the
Tree of the Knowledge of Good and Evil
found in the Garden of Eden.

Some quilts are strongly individual and obviously the work of women who wanted to extend the boundaries of conventionality (See illustrations no. 48 and 49). Miss Sally Bohannon's mother made such a quilt in Greeneville about 1850 (See illustrations no. 50 and 51). The Tree of Life is the name given by its owner, Lucille Bohannon, Miss Sally's niece. Bold, forceful green trees with three pairs of opposite branches are applied to 17-inch blocks. The branches bear plump fruit, presumably apples, in a startling combination of orange, red, and pink. Eleven of the blocks have identical placement of fruit, and each tree is topped with four leaves. The twelfth block, at the upper right hand corner, has a totally different arrangement of fruit, with two apples and four leaves in close proximity at the center top. The blocks are set with bright orange and white bands of Wild Goose Chase design in double rows. Two borders are the same as the set, while the other two have an added row of geese in sparkling pink. If Mrs. Bohannon's quilt gives insight into her personality, she must have been a purposeful woman who was not given to conformity.

While it was common practice for nineteenth-century quiltmakers to vary standard patterns to their liking, few truly original quilts were found in the study. Baskets and urns of flowers had variations from quilt to quilt, but as a body they looked more alike than different. The same can be said for the numerous rose patterns. It seems that a rose is a rose.

The opportunity to produce a quilt of unique origin is unlimited in making an applique quilt. In a pieced quilt the design is bound by the geometric units that must fit together. The laid-on work of applique has no restrictions. Any shape can be placed on background material, and only a modicum of ingenuity and skill is required to cut interesting shapes. Freedom can be intimidating, however, and conventionality appears to have inhibited Tennessee's quiltmakers from being very original. We found invention rare in the survey.

Three applique quilts stand out from the others in this respect. They have a quality of sameness; yet each is distinct. The units vary from ten inches to thirty-two inches in the size of the squares. All three designs were cut from red and green fabric (the green has faded) and applied to a white background. The intricacy of the cutting is varied, but similar, from one to the other. The level of accomplishment indicates the hand of a person or persons experienced in the art of folded-paper cutting. These are the Peddler quilts. Florence Peto has described a similar quilt in *American Quilts and Coverlets.*[21]

The peddler's wagon, or rolling store, was a great convenience to southern agrarian families. The arrival of the peddler was an exciting event. Housewives saved produce for barter or pennies for making purchases when he arrived with practical and frivolous supplies. First baking soda, then thread, and maybe a length of calico were carefully selected. Other sewing and household articles were examined. The same peddler appeared with regularity and became well acquainted with his customers.

The late Ollie McBrayer recalled several years ago in Chattanooga the visit a peddler made to her father, J. M. Miller, about 1885.

"Mama and Papa were good about taking in peddlers for meals. One poor old fellow who came around was Jeppie Parmer. He carried his wares, pots and pans and other light goods, on his back and went from house to house. He was always barefoot, even in winter. Asked to stay to dinner one day, he shyly sat down on the end of a long bench. The other end flew up, flipping him back into the corner and nearly into the flour barrel. We thought it was very funny and laughed until we cried. Papa, who was always very courteous and kind, was embarrassed for the poor thing and made us hush. He said we'd have to leave the table if we didn't behave."[22]

## [52] PEDDLER'S QUILT.

*Maker:* Fannie Steele.
   Shelbyville, Bedford County, 1865.
*Owner:* Knox Pitts, whose wife was
   Mildred Pitts, great-niece of Miss Steele.
*Applique:* 98½" x 93"; cotton: red, green
   (faded), yellow-orange, white; white
   muslin back; red binding on the straight;
   leaves and circles quilted, 13 stitches to
   the inch, in the background; stuffed
   from the top under applique pieces.

The intricate applique work put on with
the tiniest of whipped stitches is a model of
diligence. The peddler who cut the paper
design for Miss Steele had the easiest part.

53

[53] Detail of number 52.

Two decades earlier, about 1865, a peddler made his rounds in the Shelbyville area in Bedford County, stopping at the home of P. C. Steele on Midland Road. He asked to spend the night at the Steeles' house and next morning offered to pay for his night's lodging. Mr. Steele generously refused payment. In return, as a gift for kind hospitality, the peddler cut out three quilt designs for his host's daughter, Fannie Steele. Fannie spent many hours stitching the elaborate pieces to the background and even pushed extra stuffing under the cutout pieces. The quilting is in finely-stitched circles and leaves. Fannie's quilt (See illustrations no. 52 and 53) passed down to her great-niece, the late Mildred Steele Pitts.

The second peddler quilt in our survey was found in Henry County, about 150 miles northwest of Shelbyville. According to its owner, Peggy Wimberley Hall, the quilt was made some time between 1860 and 1870 in Henry County by her great-grandmother, Arminta Byers Cox. Family history credits a peddler with "pinching out" the pattern for its maker. Mrs. Cox's quilt has five large motifs appliqued to a wholecloth top. Two half-blocks fill in each side. The cutout pieces are red cotton. One spear-like shape emerges from the side of each of the cutouts. These are tan, probably faded from original green. The quilting is done in allover 3/4 inch rows.

The third quilt has not been identified as a peddler quilt, but its similarity to the other two is marked. It was made by Martha Paralee Simmons Burton, probably in Henry County, about 1855 or 1860. The cutting is more complicated and larger in scale, one unit filling a 35-inch square, of which there are four. Each cutting is of green material with a single red flower in the center and four red buds at the outer edge. The background is quilted in allover 1/2-inch diamonds. The quilt has been passed down in the Burton family to Martha's grandson, Almon, who gave it to his step-granddaughter, Peggy Lamkins Craig.

In addition to finding comparisons such as these, a number of interesting coincidences occurred. When the same type of quilting was noticed on two different sets of quilts, it turned out that unacquainted distant relatives had brought them. Several times identical or similar quilts appeared on the same day, not to appear again during the survey. If the makers were not related, it seems likely that they were friends and had the same pattern source. Certain fads arose in quilt-making that sometimes occurred in only one place, as, for example, the stuffed quilts of Rhea County.

*Nan Kinkead came home to Hawkins County in 1856 to teach school after graduating from Holston Conference Female College in Asheville, North Carolina. She made a Rocky Mountain Road quilt for her dowry before the Civil War started but marriage was delayed and she was past thirty before she became a bride.*
*—From family records of Maryana S. Huff*

**[54] DOUBLE IRISH CHAIN.**

*Maker:* Eleanor Wilson Broyles.
*Signed:* "Enoch '86"
  Rhea Springs, Rhea County, 1886.
*Lender:* Bettye J. Broyles,
  great-granddaughter.
*Pieced:* 81¼" x 72"; cotton: solid red and
  pink, white; handwoven coarse white
  back; straight white cotton binding
  machine applied; quilted and stuffed
  vases of flowers in plain areas with ¼"
  rows of quilting in background, ½"
  diagonal rows in pieced areas.

Mrs. Broyles made this quilt for her son
Enoch when she was fifty-eight, at a time
when many stuffed quilts were being
produced in Rhea County. She made at
least one quilt for each of her five children
for their marriages. The elaborate patterns
for quilting and stuffing were not reserved
for applique quilts alone, as this quilt
indicates. The classic dignity of the Irish
Chain provides a suitable frame for the
delicate quilting motif.

[55] Full view of number 54.

[56] Enoch C. Broyles and his wife, Margaret. Quilt was made for him in 1886.

According to Patsy and Myron Orlofsky in *Quilts in America*, the stuffing technique was practiced in the late eighteenth and early nineteenth centuries. A coarse backing of homespun or other loose material was used to facilitate the process. After the quilting was completed, the quilt was turned over and additional cotton or wool was forced into the quilted motifs with a bodkin, stiletto, or thorn.[23] The leaves, flowers, or feathers thus stuffed would stand higher than the rest of the quilt. Even as simple a pattern as Irish Chain could become glamorous with the addition of a stuffed urn of flowers (See illustrations no. 55 and 56). These quilts were cherished by their makers because of the painstaking care that went into their making. They remain works of great beauty.

**[57] TRENTHAM QUILT** (Similar to Chestnut Bud or Pineapple).

*Maker:* Mary A. Trentham & Nancy Jane Trentham.
  Spring City, Rhea County, 1881.
*Lender:* The family of Randolph M. and JoAn T. Trentham.
*Pieced & Applique:* 89½″ x 73¼″; cotton: pink and red print calico, faded green, yellow, and red, possibly home dyed; white background; white handwoven cotton back; white binding on the straight; quilting includes wreaths, garlands, grapes, and handprints. Stipple quilting is in the background of the applique motifs.

Mary A. Trentham, born in 1857 in Rhea County, made the quilt after she was married. Nancy Jane Trentham (her sister-in-law), born in 1840, helped with the quilting. When Mary's one-year-old daughter Nanny was trying to interrupt the quilting, the woman decided to draw around Nanny's little hands and quilted the designs into the top of the quilt. From that time on, it was considered to be Nanny's quilt.

[58] Full view of number 57.

[59] Nannie Trentham, whose hand outlines at the age of one were quilted into the surface of the quilt.

[60] Quiltmaker, Mary Ann Walker Trentham.

59

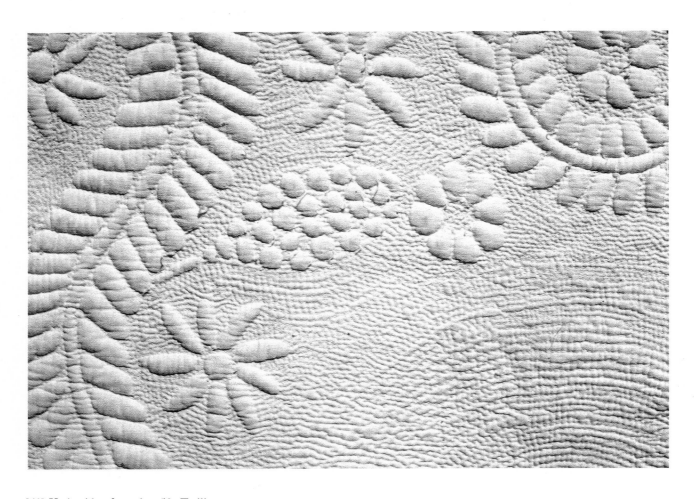

[**61**] Underside of number 58. Trailings
of cotton are visible where quilt was
stuffed.

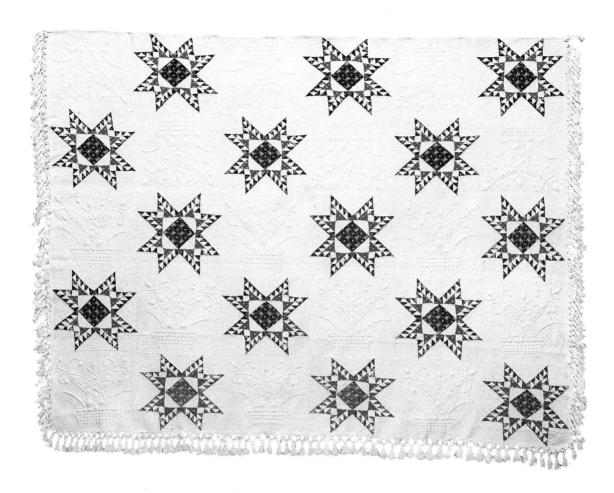

The survey team saw a few elaborately stuffed quilts on earlier quilt days. After documenting sixty-six quilts in Dayton on a Labor Day weekend and finding twenty of them to be stuffed, we declared Rhea County to be the stuffing capital of Tennessee. Rhea County lies in the fertile valley to the west of the Tennessee River as it flows from Kingston to Chattanooga. It is an area well-suited to agriculture, and early settlers coming by river quickly claimed it. The farms prospered, and the towns of Dayton and Spring City grew into small commercial centers that served the needs of the rural county. The courthouse at Dayton is still remembered as the scene of the famous Scopes trial.

Looking back, we found that several stuffed quilts recorded in other places earlier had also been made in Rhea County. Dating was difficult because none of the quilts was signed and biographical material was sketchy, but in Rhea County the trend seems to have fallen later than that of stuffed quilts found elsewhere. It is probable that ten quilts were made before 1880, nine after, and one as late as 1910. Eleven quilts were pieced, five were wholecloth quilts, and four were applique quilts.

## [62] FEATHERED STAR.

*Maker:* Victoria Darwin Caldwell. Spring City, Rhea County, 1865.
*Lender:* Mary Heiskell Wasson, granddaughter.
*Pieced:* 85¾" x 68"; cotton: blue and red prints with a white background; back is white cotton; edge has a knotted fringe whipped to a binding on three sides of quilt; quilting, parallel diagonal rows all over except in plain blocks where a vase with flowers is quilted and stuffed.

Star patterns were found in plentiful and great variety throughout the state. The stuffing technique in this quilt is representative of quilts made in Rhea County area in the middle and late nineteenth century. The fringed border was found on very few of the surveyed quilts.

61

[**63**] Detail of number 62.

[**64**] Home of Victoria Darwin Caldwell in Spring City in 1912.

62

[65] Quiltmaker, Victoria Darwin Caldwell (r), with her sister (l) and an unidentified child.

The designs for stuffing were as varied as their patterns and ages. Of the wholecloth quilts, three made in the 1900s were divided into squares by a quilted grid of leaves or feathers. Whitework quilts made earlier in the century often have a central medallion design surrounded by bands of fancy quilting. The fourth Dayton wholecloth quilt was in this medallion style.

The pieced and applique quilts, with the exception of four, have leaves, feathers, urns, flowers, and grapes quilted and stuffed to create a bas-relief play of light and shadow. The other four have plain areas quilted in crosshatch lines to form small squares, which were then stuffed. Instead of the elegant motifs and swirling feathers, the small bumps resemble popcorn.

The strangest stuffed quilt of all was a wholecloth quilt with allover 1¼-inch squares stitched on the diagonal, with no other design. A circle the size of a penny was quilted in the center of each square and the squares were stuffed. The result was, after many hours of tedious labor, a plain grid design not much more interesting than a mattress pad.

One can speculate about the concentration of a particular type of work such as this. Quiltmakers are known to be competitive, and they don't wish to be outdone. If something is new, the eager ones will try it. Later, others will try, and the fad continues. Communities that are self-sufficient and lacking in much outside contact will continue a practice long after it has ceased in other places. Eventually the work may become a trademark, as it has in Rhea County.

*"My mother-in-law made this Double Wedding Ring quilt for my husband's 'God Knows When' chest. After we were married we used it on our bed for thirty-five years and just about wore it out."*
—Billie Dowling Aymett

The survey findings can be characterized in a general way by our impressions and more precisely by the accumulated figures already presented. We know that quiltmaking has been an essential part of most households in Tennessee. Many techniques were used, but the most popular one was piecing. Quilts were made for everyday use, special occasions, and exhibition.

The quilts of East Tennessee reflect styles of Virginia, the Carolinas, and the North more than do those of Middle and West Tennessee. However, the medallion and broderie perse quilts associated with the older states seem to have been scarce in Tennessee. Since very few early nineteenth-century quilts were brought to the quilt days, we do not have an accurate account of what may have taken place. The English template method of construction was seen very seldom.

The survey cut-off date of 1930 proved a disadvantage in documenting quilts made by black quiltmakers. While a number were brought to quilt days, more often we heard that family quilts had been lost in a fire or "used up." In recent years black women have returned to quiltmaking, but not in the same way that many of them remember from earlier days. They are no longer required to raise their own cotton or make hand-carded batts. They no longer have to strip bark for dye, use coarse thread, or depend upon scraps and wornout clothing for patchwork.

We chose our cutoff date in part to avoid certain overly-popular patterns of the 1930s and 1940s. We did not anticipate the recurrence of patterns from earlier periods ever becoming monotonous, but some came close to being so. Rose Tree, Cockscomb, Broken Star, Missouri Rose, Princess Feather, Colonial Rose, and Star of Bethlehem appeared time after time. By the 1840s and 1850s elaborately appliqued quilts were as popular here as they were in other parts of the country. Some of them seem oddly formal for use in a state that was slowly developing from wilderness territory.

[**66**] SCHOOLHOUSE.

*Maker:* Sarah Moore.
  Meigs County, circa 1920.
*Lender:* McMinn County Living Heritage
  Museum, gift of J. Howard Hornsby, Jr.,
  and family.
*Pieced:* 84¼" x 79½"; cotton: thin, in
  yellow-orange, black, gray, dark blue,
  brown, red-and-white check; cotton
  flannel back; back edge turned to front;
  tied with dark blue cotton thread.

Sarah Moore was from slave ancestry. She
worked for the Hornsby family and
produced a number of quilts.

For detail see page 104.

65

**[67] RED AND GREEN STAR**
(Rolling Star).

*Maker:* Estella Thompson Lillard.
 Nashville, Davidson County, circa 1930.
*Lender:* Anna Lillard Donelson,
 step-daughter.
*Pieced:* 79″ x 70¼″; cotton: red, dark and
 light green, white; muslin back; edge
 turned back to front; allover shell
 quilting.

Estella was a stylish dressmaker who could
make anything out of cloth. She was tall
and graceful and served as a good
advertisement for her work. She made
handsome clothes for many women of the
black community, as well as making
curtains and slipcovers. "She was a
seamstress from the heart," says Mrs.
Donelson. She learned her quiltmaking
skills from her mother and enjoyed going
to her house whenever there was a quilting
group gathered. Estella's quilts reflect her
love for fabric.

66

[**68**] Quiltmaker, Estella Thompson Lillard.

We expected to find certain patterns in greater numbers than we did. The Fleur-de-Lis design popular in Maryland and Pennsylvania[24] was documented only once. The Oak Leaf and Reel, thought to be one of the standard old patterns,[25] was recorded four times. The eagle motif that dominates Pennsylvania quiltmaking designs[26] appeared a single time in a wholecloth whitework quilt. Log Cabin quilts in several variations and arrangements were fewer than expected (25) when compared with the number of crazy quilts recorded (78).

[**69**] Detail of number 70.

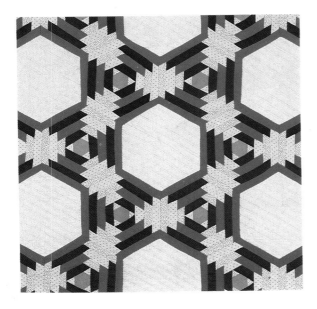

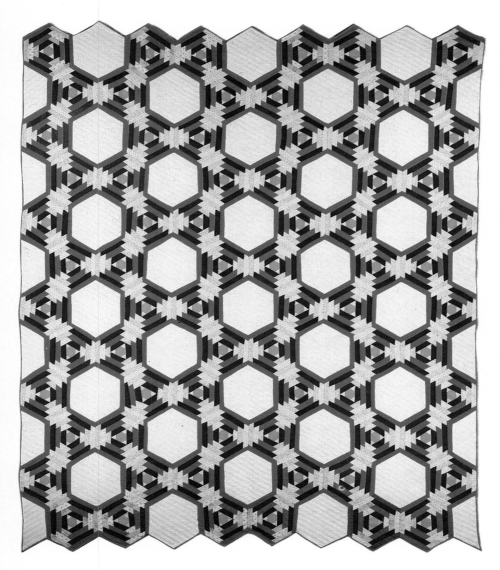

## [70] MILKY WAY

*Makers:* Nancy Jane Patterson Cope and
 Drucilla Greer Cope.
 Palestine Community, Henry County,
 circa 1880.
*Lender:* Emily Daniel Cox,
 great-granddaughter and granddaughter.
*Pieced:* 95" x 80"; cotton: red, green, white
 prints, yellow solid; no backing, coarse
 white cotton foundation for pieced and
 plain blocks; red binding; plain blocks
 are quilted by machine in double parallel
 rows.

The plain hexagon blocks were quilted
before being joined to the pieced hexagons
in a quilt-as-you-go method. Mrs. Cope
and her daughter lived together and
enjoyed many years of cooperative
quiltmaking. Mrs. Cox inherited a houseful
of quilts, coverlets, and handmade articles.

On the other hand, there were quilts that were "discoveries," ones
that we had never encountered. According to Barbara Brackman in
ongoing correspondence, our mystery quilts are no better known in
other parts of the country. An intricately pieced Sunburst quilt (See
illustration no. 71) in essentially the same pattern, with slight variations, was documented three times. A similar quilt, made in the mid-
nineteenth century by a woman from Georgia, was brought to the
Texas survey and was claimed to be an original design by its present
owner. Later another quilt of this design appeared at the Texas documentation.[27] Two other examples of this pattern have been seen on
other occasions not connected with the survey, but the mystery of the
origin of the pattern continues.[28] Two quilts of unknown pieced patterns were brought to the Jonesborough quilt day, and a third appeared in Dayton. One of the quilt owners called her quilt Taylor's
Victory, a name which may refer to several Taylors involved in political contests and controversies in the state.

## [71] SUNBURST.

*Maker:* Mary Hutton Rankin.
*Signed:* "Mary Hutton May 20, 1850."
Bedford County.
*Owners:* Mr. and Mrs. Arthur Rankin, Jr.,
great-great-grandson.
*Pieced:* 99″ x 86″; cotton: red, green,
white; handwoven white back; red
dotted binding added; quilted by the
piece and double shells in the
background.

Precise piecing, fine quilting, and a
well-composed arrangement of blocks
combine to make an exceptional quilt.

## [72] FRIENDSHIP.

*Maker:* Elizabeth Mathews Baxter.
Rocky Flats Community, Cocke County,
1871.
*Lender:* Newport-Cocke County Museum,
gift of Eldridge Baxter Smelcer, Ola
Baxter Thomas, Willie Ruth Baxter
Williams, Judy Baxter Wright, and
Jeffery Baxter Wright, descendants.
*Pieced:* 81¼″ x 64¼″; cotton: brown &
white stripe, assorted calico; set blocks
are pink and red calico; white back;
binding of indigo resist print; quilting is
by the piece in the pieced blocks and
diamond quilting in the plain blocks.

Elizabeth Baxter made the quilt as a
wedding gift for her son, Robert, and his
wife, Sarah Jane Huff, in 1871. The quilt
pattern is thought to be original; it has not
been found in any of the encyclopedia of
quilt patterns. It is an excellent example of
fine piecing—the numerous points of the
blocks meet precisely. Overall, the quilt
pattern forms an optical illusion.

[73] Full view of number 72.

It has been noted that Rocky Mountain (New York Beauty) quilts are often associated with Tennessee, and justly so. The twenty-three examples we found were well-made and constructed with variety. Fourteen were arranged with blocks in vertical-horizontal position and nine on the diagonal. Three had the pieced strips embellished with appliqued serpentine rose vines in a treatment seldom seen. These three were documented in Jonesborough on the same day and had originated in three adjoining counties: Washington, Hawkins, and Sullivan.

Many of the quilts of East Tennessee are identified with white backgrounds and clear, sometimes light, colors imparting a certain elegance of style. These quilts seem to denote a consciousness of fashion and some prosperity. Those of mid-state have a more somber quality with less white and more strong, dark tones. The economic hardships of the post-Civil War period can be seen in the practical, everyday fabrics of the quilts. More emphasis seems to have been given to excellence of piecing and variety of sets, and less to fancy quilting, in Middle Tennessee. The sampling of quilts from West Tennessee was smaller; but, in general, these quilts were of strong colors and of a wider variety of prints and solids. Memphis, the commercial center for many quilters in the western part of the state, offered splendid choices of material; but in some cases the actual quilting work was much less refined than that in other areas. In the larger cities quilt fabrics tended to be more expensive, and the work was of high quality.

## [74] WHEEL OF FORTUNE

*Maker:* Margaret Ann Hall (Maggie).
  Winchester, Franklin County, 1922.
*Lender:* James Howard Hall, great-nephew.
*Pieced:* 88″ x 77½″; cotton: red, navy
  blue, white solids; muslin back; front
  edge turned to back; quilted by the
  piece.

Maggie made this quilt, with embroidered
name at one corner, as a wedding present
for her nephew Sam when he married Mary
Larkin. Maggie was a maiden lady who had
no place of her own after her parents died.
She spent her life moving from home to
home of relatives and friends, sometimes
staying as long as three years in one place.
She "earned her keep" by babysitting,
cooking, and performing household tasks
and was considered a valuable addition to
the family. The strong colors and style of
this quilt are characteristic of many quilts
of Middle Tennessee.

72     [75] Detail of number 74.

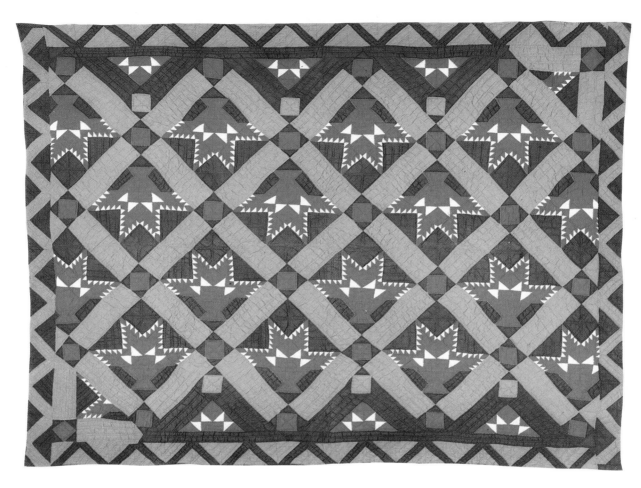

**[76] STAR IN A BASKET.**

*Maker:* Dicey Ann Bright Smith.
  Henry County, circa 1885.
*Lender:* Sue Curtis Smith,
  granddaughter-in-law.
*Pieced:* 85″ x 66½″; cotton: dark blue,
  red, white, yellow-orange; muslin back;
  front edge turned to back; quilted by the
  piece, blue and tan thread.

The maker had trouble finishing out the
corners of her quilt, for the corners are the
downfall of many quilters. (The viewer is
amused and sympathetic.) Mrs. Smith may
have worked on the quilt while recovering
from a broken hip which left her somewhat
crippled. The basket pattern has had
long-lasting popularity.

**[77] THE WORLD'S FAIR QUILT**
(Golden Splendor Variation).

*Maker:* Lillian Jackson Jones.
  Gibson County, probably 1923-24.
*Lender:* Robert B. Hicks, III,
  great-nephew.
*Pieced:* 95½″ x 75¼″; cotton: solid yellow
  and white; yellow back; yellow bias
  binding; quilted in 1″ squares,
  interlocking squares, and by the piece.

Here is a splendid example of the
1920s-1930s quilt made of high quality,
solid-colored cotton fabric, an uncluttered
design, and fine but simple quilting. Mrs.
Jones cultivated her quiltmaking ability
because she "wasn't very pretty, so I had
to have something to show for myself."
Through a national county fair competition
her quilt was judged "The best quilt in all
the 48 states and U.S. territories" and was
exhibited at the Philadelphia Fair in 1926.
Feeling there was nothing more to
accomplish, she gave up quilts for afghans
and politics. She became the first woman to
hold the position of State Voter Registrar in
Louisiana during the Huey Long
administration. She remained active in
southern politics for a number of years and
traveled to many parts of the world.

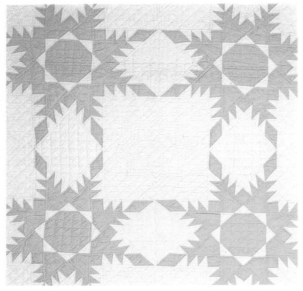

[78] Detail of number 77.

74

The palette of colors generally follows that of the rest of the country. Fabrics of certain periods can be characterized by the development of the dye industry and by the whims of fashion.[29] Tennessee quiltmakers of the 19th century made use of solid-color red, green, yellow, yellow-orange, brown, and blue cloth in combination with white, and some prints. In the 1880s brown prints were extremely popular, followed by more cheaply produced one-color prints of red, blue, or maroon with white figures. A number of the quilts documented were faded from the original colors, with red turning to brown and green turning to blue- or yellow-green. The quilt owners frequently referred to home-dyeing, either with natural dyes—walnut, maple, hickory, pokeberry, or red mud—or commercially prepared pills or packets of dye.

C olors changed radically in the twentieth century as synthetic dyes and processes were improved. The pastel look gained the attention of quiltmakers, and the shoddy cloth of the late nineteenth century was replaced with finely-woven percales and small-scale prints. Contests, fairs, printed patterns, needlework books, and good material, along with a conscious fashion of imitating colonial days,[30] combined to bring about a somewhat different era of quiltmaking—modernism. The Depression had not yet arrived.

In many ways our project parallels the work of archaeologists, who look through the remains of earlier cultures to discover what daily life was like in the cultures they study. The details of our study of quilts reveal how sturdy pioneers dependent on homegrown and homemade products emerged into a vibrant agricultural and industrial state. Linsey-woolsey and handspun, handwoven cotton materials, were gradually replaced by home-dyed commercial fabrics and store-bought prints; and then ready-made batting and wider assortments of cloth came into use. Gradually the patterns and fabric changed. In the quilts can be seen the growth of the southern textile industry which contributed in large measure to improved economic conditions. In truth, it can be said that Tennessee's history has been stitched in her quilts.

*"Papa would say, you go buy all this fabric and just sew it back together!"*
—Pauline Law Spencer

75

# NOTES

1. Cartter Patten, *A Tennessee Chronicle*, 63–81.

2. It took President Jackson more than three weeks to travel overland from the Hermitage, his home near Nashville, to the District of Columbia.

3. Interview with Mrs. Joseph A. Caldwell by Bets Ramsey, 6 May 1973, Blountville, Tennessee.

4. Laurel Horton and Lynn Robertson Myers, eds., *Social Fabric*, 11–14.

5. The Baltimore album quilt authority, Dena Katzenberg, stated in a letter of 28 February 1986, that the date seems very early to her, at a time when broderie perse and all-white quilts were being made. She would be inclined to place the date between 1850–60. It is the first time that she has heard of a Lutheran women's group making an album quilt. Katherine Shofner Anglin, great-granddaughter of Mr. Jenkins, says the quilt has been passed down in the family with the story that he brought it to Tennessee from Baltimore. Thus we have a mystery.

6. Carleton L. Safford and Robert Bishop, *America's Quilts and Coverlets*, 28–37.

7. Laurel Horton, "South Carolina Quilts in the Civil War," *Uncoverings 1985*, forthcoming.

8. In conversation, 28 September 1985 in Nashville.

9. In conversation at American Quilt Study Group conference, San Rafael, California, 12 October 1985.

10. The author observed this practice during ten years of working with Senior Neighbors of Chattanooga, Inc.

11. In conversation, 15 October 1985, San Francisco.

12. See Pat Nickols, "String Quilts," *Uncoverings 1982*, 53–57.

13. In conversation at American Quilt Study Group conference, 13 October 1985.

14. Penny McMorris, *Crazy Quilts*, 16–19.

15. See Jonathan Holstein, *The Pieced Quilt*, 185–186, n. 15.

16. A scandal associated with a former director, Virginia Wardlaw, and her two sisters may have been a contributing factor in the school's decline. In 1909 Virginia Wardlow and her sisters were convicted in New Jersey of the murder of the daughter of one of them. Stories of mystery and occultism involving the sisters lingered at the college long after they left Murfreesboro. According to Mrs. Webb, the most factual account of the scandal was given by Norman Zierold in *Three Sisters in Black*.

17. Elly Sienkiewicz, *Spoken Without A Word*, 45-46.

18. The pieced-rose technique was first noticed when the author was doing an appraisal of a quilt made in Murfreesboro about 1850. As a result, close observation was given to this type during the survey. The pattern was published in Bets Ramsey's column, "The Quilter," in the *Chattanooga Times*, 17 March 1983.

19. Florence Peto, *American Quilts and Coverlets*, 29, 36.

20. In tallying the quilts that combine piecing and applique, a minor use of either technique was disregarded. For instance, a Peony quilt that is primarily pieced but has appliqued stems is classified with pieced quilts. The Dresden Plate accounts for the major portion of this category.

21. Peto, *American Quilts*, 39-40. Also, Peto, *Historic Quilts*, xvii.

22. Interview by Bets Ramsey, 1971.

23. Patsy and Myron Orlofsky, *Quilts in America*, 186–193.

24. Gloria Seaman Allen, *Old Line Traditions*, 8, 24.

25. Marguerite Ickis, *The Standard Book of Quilt Making*, 106–108.

26. Jeannette Lasansky, *In the Heart of Pennsylvania*, 13–14.

27. Letter from Kathleen McCrady, 18 January 1986.

28. The author first saw this Sunburst pattern on Lookout Mountain in 1972 at the home of Phenie McGuffey. The quilt was made about 1870 by Sallie Boyles from a pattern she had acquired in a fortuitous way. It had dropped at her very house from a passing wagon filled with the belongings of a family moving to a new location. A second Sunburst quilt was in the possession of the late Creed Bates of Signal Mountain.

29. See Barbara Brackman, "Dating Old Quilts," *Quilter's Newsletter Magazine*, issues 165-9.

30. Allen Eaton, *Handicrafts of the Southern Highlands*, 291-292.

# QUILTING LESSONS OF *Childhood*

Ozella Angel has been a quiltmaker all her life. Since her marriage she has lived in Chattanooga, where she raised a son and a daughter and served as manager of a school cafeteria. Since retiring, she has made six Yo-Yo quilts, one for each of her grandchildren, three applique quilts of an original leaf design, and a varied dozen more. She has won several awards and has exhibited her work in art galleries and quilt shows.

When Ozella was five, her mother, Della Drummond, died at the age of thirty, leaving six children under the age of eleven. Her paternal grandmother came to rear the family. Thomas Drummond instilled the value of work and cooperation in his children by demanding that they share the load of farm and household chores. Black rural families had to work hard for a living, and life was not easy.

The two older girls learned to piece quilts from their grandmother. When Thomas saw Ozella, age seven, looking on, he asked, "What's wrong with your fingers?" It was her cue to get a thimble and begin her first lesson in piecing. She started two or three quilts before she finished her first one. The usual method was string-piecing on newspaper pattern squares. After the paper was removed, the squares were joined together to make a top.

A quilt frame was suspended from the ceiling in the main room of the Drummonds' three-room house. During the winter months, a quilt was always in the frame for the girls and their grandmother to quilt. At night the frame was raised out of the way. Ozella was taught to quilt when she was ten and then joined the others in finishing her first quilt. She had helped raise the cotton and had done her own carding for batts.

The quilts were made solely for family use out of any scraps that were available. When a top was finished, muslin sheeting or flour sacks were dyed for backing: walnut peelings for brown color, red mud for rosy red, or hickory bark for yellow. The dyeing was done

*"I started piecing quilts when I was ten. In a few years I ordered a pattern from a Nashville paper and fabric, at 11¢ a yard, from a Sears sale catalogue. That was for my Vase of Flowers quilt (c. 1930)."*
—Ora Smith Humberd

**[79] STRING STAR BLOCK.**

*Maker:* Ozella Drummond Angel,
circa 1925.

Ozella's first attempt at piecing was
string-piecing on newspaper. This star was
made at the age of seven.

*"I remember as a child in the
1920s looking forward to quilt
washing days when we would
stomp on the quilts in the bath
tub."*
—Virginia Moore Leonard of
Knoxville

outside in an iron pot. The colored backs were used on the quilts so as
not to show the soil. Five-cent ball thread was purchased with bartered eggs from the rolling store that came once a week. It was un-
thinkable to buy cloth for quilts, but by selling eggs and chickens one
earned enough credit for a dress length, from which there were scraps
which could be used.

The small farm house was cold in winter when snow and rain blew
in the cracks. There were no inner ceilings and no insulation under
the floor, below which the chickens and hogs were sheltered. Quilts
were a major concern for the cold months. Ozella made a Cocklebur
quilt for the boys, which pleased them and served them well because
of its thickness. She cut the pieces out of their old overalls and work-
clothes. In assembling her quilt, she used a method of folding a
square in half diagonally and then bringing the diagonal edges together to form a pointed shape.[1] Starting in the center of a firm piece
of backing, she sewed overlapping rows of points together in concentric circles.

The Drummond children attended a one-room school for three
months in winter and two in summer, along with thirty-five other
children. They completed the six grades offered, but their father was
unable to send them to boarding school in town for further education.

Ozella continued to live at home, work in the field, keep house,
quilt, and learn other needlework. With some of the family gone, she
had more time to try out new quilt patterns and exchange scraps with
friends. Eventually the right man asked her to marry, and she left her
family to begin her own. She is glad that her children have had educa-
tional and professional advantages and that her grandchildren have
been spared her hardships, but she is satisfied that her up-bringing
was profitable.[2]

Ozella's white counterpart, Bernice Schultz Mackey, did not have
to be pushed into sewing. When she was eight years old, she began
making doll clothes on Saturday afternoons while her mother was
shopping in town. Tootsie, as she was called, was too small to sit on a
chair and use the sewing machine; so she stood, pushing the treadle
with one foot. She would "borrow" material from her mother's quiltmaking supply. When her mother complained that she couldn't keep
any material for quilts, Tootsie replied that her dolls had to have
something to wear.

Mrs. Schultz predicted that Tootsie would surely sew her finger
someday, but she never forbade the use of the sewing machine. One
day the expected did happen, and Tootsie quickly turned the wheel to
release the needle from her finger. Then she ran to the coal oil can to
immerse her finger in coal oil, the standard household remedy. After
the finger was healed, she told her mother about the accident, but she
continued to sew.

Finally, Tootsie was told that if she must sew, she could have some
material for a quilt. Since she could sew so well, she didn't have to
start with the usual beginner's Nine Patch. She cut 1-inch squares for
her version of Trip Around the World. Eventually she completed
twenty-one blocks, with 184 pieces in each block, and set them together with alternating squares of plain blue.

## [80] TRIP AROUND THE WORLD
(My Hard Times Quilt).

*Maker:* Bernice Schultz Mackey (Tootsie).
  Athens, McMinn County, 1927, started.
*Lender:* Elyssa Hood Clayton, great-niece.
*Pieced:* 78½" x 71"; cotton: assorted scraps
  set with blue; muslin feed-sack back;
  front edge turned to back; quilted in
  diagonal rows and squares.

Tootsie Schultz was twelve years old when
she started her version of the Trip Around
the World. She used twenty-one miniature
blocks set together with plain blocks.
There are 184 one-inch pieces in each
block.

[81] Detail of number 80.

79

[82] Quiltmaker, Bernice Shultz, in 1929.
She began piecing her Hard Times Quilt in
1927.

Tootsie calls this her Hard Times quilt because, although it was started in 1927, it was finished during the Depression when families economized in every way possible. Her mother made use of the cloth from the 100-pound bags of feed she bought for her large flock of chickens. When empty, the bags were washed and made into quilt linings, sheets, and pillowcases. The Hard Times quilt is backed with a feed-sack lining.[3]

Bernice Mackey spent a number of years caring for sick families and babies before marrying rather late in life. Following the death of her husband, she has returned to the comfort of sewing. She helped make a trousseau for a great-niece, and she makes doll clothes for two great-great-nieces. She smocks and makes her own clothes and has never lost her love for making quilts.[4] A little girl called Tootsie learned her lessons well.

## NOTES

1. Squares folded into points are also called Prairie Points.
2. Interview with Ozella Angel by Bets Ramsey, Chattanooga, 20 January 1986.
3. From a letter written by Bernice Mackey to her great-niece, Elyssa Hood Clayton, owner of the Hard Times quilt, 30 December 1985.
4. Letter to author from Caroline Hood, 16 February 1986.

# NEWS FAR AND NEAR: *The Blair Quilts*

The quilt historian can be grateful for the Blair sisters of Roane County, Tennessee. While most objects from the past are lost to us, and almost all paper, these women of the late 1800s saved cloth, paper receipts, tools, bottles, clothes, linens, photographs, letters, newspapers, and magazines. A family tradition even says that they saved the string used to tie the youngest daughter's navel cord.

The Blair sisters were great-aunts of Mary Johnson Browning and her sister Reba Johnson White, who brought eleven quilts to our documentation session at the McMinn County Living Heritage Museum on November 30, 1984. The quilts themselves, like most quilts, provided physical data of importance for our research; but it was exciting to learn that they owned ledger sheets and family letters which told of what went into the quilts and of the women who made them.

The eleven quilts that Mary Browning and Reba White brought to the session consisted of two pieced Rose of Sharon, one applique Tulip, two Double Irish Chain, two linsey quilts—one in the Streak of Lightning pattern, one in the Bar pattern—one Goose Tracks variation, one sampler of quilt blocks, one Star of the East, and one Basket of Scraps. All these types were frequent in the nineteenth century in Tennessee. These fabrics and colors are also typical of Tennessee quilts. Several are made of purchased calicoes: the pieced Rose of Sharon, yellow, deep rose, and green; the Star of the East, brown and rust; the two Double Irish Chains, navy blue, pink, and rose. The Streak of Lightning and Bar quilts are made of a coarse handwoven linsey fabric. (Linsey is a fabric in which wool is woven into a linen or cotton warp.) The Basket of Scraps is, as its name implies, made of sewing scraps.

The quilting techniques are also typical. Both Rose of Sharon quilts are "best" quilts, with floral motifs quilted into the plain white areas and parallel lines (eight stitches to the inch) quilted ¼-inch apart through the block and border areas. The linsey quilts have the crudest quilting, with only four stitches to the inch in parallel rows ¾-inch

*"I have made John a nice new jeans coat and lined it all over with linsey. He is all right for jack frost."*
—Harriet Blair, 1882

81

[83] BASKET OF SCRAPS.

*Maker:* The Blair Sisters—Susan, Mary
  Ann or Elizabeth Jane.
  Barnardsville, Roane County, circa 1880.
*Lender:* Mary Johnson Browning,
  great-niece.
*Pieced:* 84″ x 73″; cotton: assorted calico
  prints in red, brown and blue; the set
  blocks are brown calico with brown and
  black dots; white muslin back; unbound;
  batting is handcarded cotton; quilting is
  in parallel rows ½″ apart running
  horizontally across the surface.

The Blair sisters did sewing for others in
the community. This quilt is made of many
sewing scraps and probably contains fabric
swatches from friends living in other states.
The letters left at the farm often include
requests for dress scraps for quilting
projects. (See article for further
information.)

82

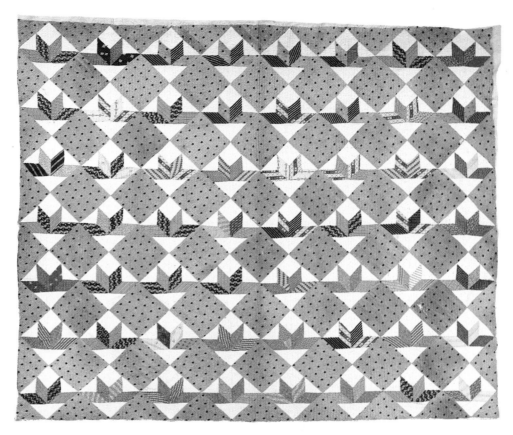

[84] Full view of number 83.

apart. This is typical for linsey since the handwoven top fabric, the batting, and the backing fabric are very thick. The other pieced quilts have parallel lines or diamonds quilted over their surfaces.

The quilts are typical enough for us to be sure of their patterns and fairly sure of the dates they were made (second half of the nineteenth century). The material tells something about the lives of the people. The Basket of Scraps quilt has unbound edges, making visible the inconsistent quality of the cotton batting. This suggests hand carding. Hand carding was done with raw cotton; hence the farm was likely to have grown its own cotton. But they obviously had some money, too; for the commercially-printed calicoes were fine fabrics.

Mary Browning lives, as did her family (including her great-aunts, the Blair sisters), on a farm ten miles from Kingston in Roane County, a lush agricultural area of East Tennessee. At the time the quilts were made, the community around the farm was called Barnardsville. The farm still has three of the original hand-hewed log buildings. At one time there may have been as many as thirty-six buildings, including a main house, a smokehouse, a buggy shed, a crib, barns, a loom house, a tannery, hen houses, a workshop, a granary, a springhouse, and a separate kitchen. The remaining tools, materials, letters, photographs, and printed records tell us much about the Blair farm and its occupants.

[85] Artifacts found on the farm which once belonged to the Blair family of Roane County: calico sewing scraps found in some of the quilts, a scrap of checked linsey, portions of hand-sewn garments, skeins of cotton and flax, a letter proposing marriage to Mary Ann Blair, and calling cards for Susan Blair, Nancy Blair and their mother, Mary Blair. (Still life arranged by Margaret Luttrell.)

The Blair family was neither poor nor rich. Of Scotch-Irish background, they descended from the Hugh Blair family who, after leaving Ireland following the rebellion, settled in Lancaster County, Pennsylvania, in 1746 and later moved to Guilford County, North Carolina in 1771. Three generations later the John Blair family began farming in Roane County, Tennessee.[1] The property (273 acres in 1868)[2] owned by John Blair (1809–1886) was valued at $2,200 in 1868.[3] He worked as a tanner as well as a farmer, making such leather items as shoes, saddles, horse collars, belts, and book covers. The ledger listing the price he charged for each item is extant. His wife, Mary Blair (1813-1876), was a daughter of Thomas and Mary Johnson, wealthy farmers who owned much land and several slaves. The Blairs had a few slaves; there are sales receipts for two of them— Charly, bought for $1,150 in 1853[4] and Edward, bought for $1,750 in 1863.[5]

The five Blair sons included Samuel Thomas Blair (1833–1880) and James Washington Blair (1849–1910). Of the four Blair daughters, three never married. Mary Ann (1836–1910) was shy and a hard worker. Elizabeth Jane (1841–1920) was of quick temper and wit; she loved caring for the cattle and, according to family tradition, once built a privy. Susan Caroline Blair (1846–1924), called "Sookie," was a homebody, spending her time doing housework, cooking, and sewing.[6]

Nancy (1852–1886), the youngest of the daughters, married George Johnson. Her only son, John Edgar Levi Johnson, was two years old when she died at the age of thirty-four. The three unmarried sisters raised him on the farm. John, who died in 1981 at the age of ninety-seven, was the father of Mary Johnson Browning, the current owner of the farm and one of two sisters who brought the quilts to the documentation session.

John Blair, the father, was a Union sympathizer, as were most citizens of Roane County.[7] He was the postmaster; the post office was in the front room of the main house.[8] He was active in the county court, serving as a Revenue Commissioner for the Tenth District of Roane County.[9] Apparently, in that capacity he collected fees for schoolteachers, since his records show those fees: students in the first grade paid the teacher $1.00 per month, those in the second grade paid $1.50, those in the third grade and higher paid $2.00.[10] The subjects taught in 1861 were orthography, philosophy, astronomy, reading, writing, arithmetic, geography, English grammar, algebra, and physiology.[11] The Blair records show that in 1868, and hence probably for a good while before and after, white and black children attended Oak Hill School.[12]

The Blair women also had paying jobs at home. The mother and the four daughters, according to family tradition, did weaving and sewing for others in the community, as well as for themselves. Among the Blair papers are dated store receipts showing type, amount, and costs of purchases. A statement dated 1873 from the W. J. Betterton Company includes a large amount of fabric:

| | | | |
|---|---|---|---|
| 7 | yards calico | .10 | .70 |
| 59½ | yards do[a] | .11¹/² | 6.83 |
| 9 | [?] paper Cambrick | .15 | 1.35 |
| 1 | ps Bk Domestic[b] for | | 7.00 |
| 35½ | yds Bro do | .10 | 3.55 |
| 6 | yds Velvet | | .50 |
| 3 | Bunches Braid | | .15 |
| 26 | yds Black Calico | .11½ | 2.99 |
| 28 | Doz 700 Thread | .15 | 4.20 |
| 21 | Doz 500 do | .20 | 4.20[13] |

[a]do means "ditto"      [b]Domestic is muslin

The quantities approach the astonishing, suggesting that the Blair sisters were mercers—reselling fabric and notions—did much sewing for others, or were dedicated quilters.

The statement also tells of work and pleasure on the farm, including spirits of turpentine, nails, putty, shot, rope, a handsawfile, collars, a shawl, a bowl and pitcher, a soap stand, teaspoons, candy, two plugs of tobacco, a jug, and a gallon of BB Whiskey.

An 1861 statement of the account of John Blair and his son, S. T. Blair, with McEwen & Hornsby, a store in nearby Kingston, lists:

| | |
|---|---|
| For 6 yd Domestic @ 9 | .75 |
| For 8 yd yellow Flannel @ .60 | 4.80 |
| For 9 yd Bedticking & ⅙ Gum Camphor .10 | 2.35[14] |

Also included were purchases for the tannery business: shoepegs and shoerasps. The year's purchases were bartered for eighteen horse collars and a side of upper leather.

Other receipts tell us of domestic, medical and farm life, including purchases of camphor, pills, nutmeg, cinnamon, salt, window glass, shears, a looking glass, a scythe blade, and a cane mill.

[**87**] The Blair sisters, seated left to right,
Susan Caroline and Elizabeth Jane.
Standing: Mary Ann and their nephew,
J. E. L. Johnson, in front of farmhouse in
Roane County in 1900.

The quilt patterns of the Blair quilts are found throughout the Eastern United States and Canada, strongly suggesting wide communication. How the communication took place and the geographical paths it traveled are more difficult to tell, although some of it was undoubtedly through magazines and newspapers. *Comfort Magazine*, published in Augusta, Maine, offered as a motto "The Key to Million and Quarter Homes."[15] One of those homes was the Blair home, which still has several years of issues from the late nineteenth and early twentieth centuries. The magazine contained regular features on palmreading, craft projects, recipes, and advice to the lovelorn; and it was well known for quilt patterns, even though the copies from 1895 to 1900 at the Blair home happen to contain none. Other magazines include a July 25, 1868 issue of *Harper's Bazar* [sic] which contained a feature on the manufacture of calico,[16] and a January, 1901 issue of *Home Monthly* carrying a mail order advertisement for quilt patterns from the Ladies Art Company of Saint Louis, Missouri, in a style to be remembered: "Every quilter should have our book of 400 designs, containing the prettiest, queerest, most grotesque, scarcest patterns, from old log cabin to stars and puzzle designs; unique, beautiful; including 100 crazy stitches."[17]

Also very important for this family, as for many Tennesseans, were the rivers. One historical account of the area points out that "perhaps the most important single influence on Kingston's social and economic development was the rivers which surrounded it . . . it derived much of its importance during the nineteenth century from its strategic location along the upper Tennessee River . . . the bend in the Clinch River near its mouth at Kingston was the best natural port anywhere on the upper Tennessee River."[18]

The rivers touched the lives of the family in an important way in 1878, when a letter from the Domestic Sewing Machine Company in Richmond, Virginia requested whether the Blairs planned to buy the sewing machine about which they had inquired.[19] They did buy the sewing machine, which came by river. A steamboat bill of lading dated 1878 includes the Domestic Sewing Machine and other receipts for purchases.

Weaving fabric for clothing and bed linens was common in homes of nineteenth-century Tennessee families.[20] The Blair women wove many fine coverlets which have been documented in Sadye Tune Wilson and Doris Kennedy's book, *Of Coverlets: The Legacies, The Weavers*.[21] The Blair women also wove fabric for garments, a number of which survive. The fabric was linsey, a fabric found in two of the Blair quilts. A number of quilt owners at our quilt documentation days spoke of seeing tattered linsey quilts in the tobacco shed or in the barn covering the tractor. Since most of the fabric in these quilts was made on the farm, such quilts are very much true Tennessee quilts. (See illustration no. 89 for an example of a linsey quilt.)

The Blair farm still contains evidence of the sewing and weaving done in earlier generations: a spinning wheel, a flax wheel, skeins of

[88] James and Harriet Blair of Bentonville, Arkansas.

linen and cotton, carding implements, and a yarn winder. These are all the tools needed to produce handwoven cloth, except for the loom, which was sold and may very well be the loom on display in the Kingston Courthouse. Also surviving are garments made of handwoven linsey: several skirts, a dress with a long skirt, and a blue jean[22] jacket lined with a checked linsey. The quilts and the clothes, the people and the labor, the farm and the family—the historian is concerned with all. The Blair family records, artifacts, and quilts open windows to the past, not only of the Blair sisters, but of Tennesseans and Americans elsewhere.

In the old granary building there is still some commercial fabric on bolts, one of which has an advertising sticker with the name of "Wm. Simpson & Son, Philadelphia." There are also large pieces of cloth in solids of black and brown, lengths of cotton flannel, and a piece of brown cambric. Finally, there are smaller amounts of fabric in calico prints, some of which appear in several of the Blair quilts.

Since most of the Blair quilts use only one or two fabrics throughout, it is clear that the makers probably planned in advance and purchased the fabric specifically for a quilt project, as many twentieth-century quilters do.

Although the Basket of Scraps quilt (See illustration no. 83) contains the same fabric in the plain blocks, the flower and basket sections of the pieced blocks are made of a variety of multicolored calico prints, suggesting that sewing scraps were used. Letters from Arkansas, mention the sending of pieces of fabric from Arkansas to Tennessee and Tennessee to Arkansas.

The most delightful discovery we made at the Blair farm was the letters to the Blair sisters from their sister-in-law, lighthearted accounts of a young couple and their five children in their new life in Arkansas. The letters tell us of daily living, of pluck and good humor, and of quilting.

James Washington Blair and his wife Harriet moved to Bentonville, Arkansas, in 1882. John Blair helped his son James purchase the property. Harriet, who was trained to be a schoolteacher, wrote well and observantly, and the letters from her children offer a lively and often amusing perspective.

In a letter dated December 10, 1882, Harriet wrote:

> "The children want me to write some for them. Mary says to tell her Aunts that she picked dried beans and sold enough to buy her a nice worsted dress, and concluded we would not make up the one you gave her until she is a little older. I have made John [one of her sons] a nice new jeans coat and lined it all over with linsey. He is all right for jack frost. . . .
>
> "Excuse bad writing for Dannie [her then two-year-old] is at my elbow punching me for the pencil, write me all the news far and near. . . ."

In a postscript she adds, "Girls, please write me how you make calico and worsted dresses in Tennessee. I do not like the fashions here, write how to make them for children."[23]

In a letter dated April 9, 1883, Harriet's daughter, Mary, shows some initiative and some self-satisfaction.

> "Ma and Pa stays to home and works and makes us too, but I study my lessons every day. I have been thru my third reader three times, spelled all the spelling by heart. So Ma has now put me in a larger reader, one that Pa used to read in at school. Tell Aunt Nancy I was going to try my luck raising geese. I have some eggs setting. I think maybe by age 21 I will have me a feather bed. I am piecing me a very pretty scrap quilt called Winding Blades. I can crochet, please send me some little pieces of crocheting for a sample. I want to make some pretty trimming for mine and Maggie's pantiletts."[24]

On May 20, 1883, Harriet wrote, "I am making butter every week . . . and I sell it all at the nearby stores and have been clothing the entire family for six months or longer just with the cows, and now you have no idea what it takes for a growing family every day and Sunday ware."[25]

On January 25, 1885, Maggie, the then six-year-old daughter, wrote a note to cheer her grandpa who was sick with cancer.

> "I am over to horseback in spelling book, just learning at home and now I am piecing me a quilt, I have 12 stars done, nearly all of the pieces were scraps that the neighbor girls have give to me, so just please send me a piece of one of your shirts and my aunties' a piece of one of their dresses to put in my quilt and I will send you a piece of my new dress. Dannie [then four] says to write to me and him like you do to John and Mary."[26]

On January 25, 1885, Mary wrote to her grandpa about her success in school.

"I have thirty-six head marks for being head in my spelling class . . . I received a prize for being head. . . . I do want Aunt Nancy's sweet little babe's picture worse than anything in the world. You must not give it all your love. There is five little children in Arkansas that love you and talk about you everyday. Please tell Aunt Nancy to send me a little of John Edgar Lee Johnson's [the newborn baby's] dresses, just to look at."[27]

On July 20, 1890, Harriet wrote, "I have up a quilt now that Maggie [then 11] pieced. Have quilted two already and have four more to quilt this fall. They are comforts. Susan I must tell you that Maggie is just the nicest and fastest quilter you ever saw for her age. It would surprise you to see how much she will get done and that well done too in an afternoon."[28]

The letters from Arkansas remind, inform, and amuse. One letter from Alabama both amuses and saddens. At least one of the three unmarried Blair sisters did not lack for a suitor. In a letter dated March 3, 1861, from Newmarket, Alabama, Mark H. Taliaferro offered his hand and heart to Mary Ann Blair. One may wonder how she resisted such tender and thoughtful words.

[89] The James Blair family of Arkansas. From left: Sammie, Maggie, James, Dannie, John, Harriet, Mary, and unidentified child. Photo taken circa. 1895.

"Well, Miss Mary Ann B, I am sure you are astonished at me; But let this be as it may, I will write you a letter today. Madam, I have been trying for some time to persuade myself that it was useless for me to say anything to you but some how or other I cannot be satisfied without saying something I do not know exactly what it will be. Time would fail me to tell you how many times I have been disappointed, so it will not go hard with me, this letter or none again to see. Madam I would like to know if you could admire such an erring creature as myself and if you could be persuaded to leave the State of Tennessee, I am standing in need of a assistant in my school and would like to have some to cheer me during my lonely hours as I am a stranger in a strange land. One to share my bitters and sweets, but alas madam none to quarrel or scold. None to turn a cold look, but I want a smiling countenance a cheerful heart one that looks to the happiness of others, yes one that will not let passion govern, but on the contrary governs passion by reason. Now if you think you can fill the bill, it would be agreeable to my will. If not say out right, and we will neither quarrel nor fight."[29]

Sewing continued, along with joys and sadness. In a letter dated January 27, 1924, from Gary, Indiana, Dan Blair (the son of James and Harriet Blair, now grown up to be an engineer with a family) expresses to his cousin "Johnnie" [John Edgar Levi Johnson] his sadness on hearing of the death of his Aunt Susan Blair, the last of the Blair sisters.

"I am certainly sorry I didn't get to see Aunt Susan. I had written sister the first of January telling her I was going to see Aunt Susan Blair in June and from there to see Mother in Arkansas. Yes, I knew she had a coverlet for me. If I had known she was going to be sick and die, I would have gone anyway to see her."

Later in the same letter Dan Blair expresses a concern of the times: "I hope you stay there on the farm . . . don't let anyone get it from you."[30]

John Edgar Levi Johnson stayed on the farm and married Cora Galyon. They reared two sons, John Coolidge and Donald Spencer, and two daughters, Reba Lois and Mary Ruth. Until his death in 1981 at the age of 97, J. E. L. Johnson maintained the records and artifacts left by the Blair sisters. In his will dated 22 September 1969 he writes:

"As to old records of which I have some dating back to the Resolution [sic] Period and old books, I request that my children not to destroy them, but to keep them in tact and I have asked my daughter, Mary Johnson Browning is [sic] she would take these records and keep them in tact for me . . . I feel they will have some value if not a great value in the future, and that many people might get information that they want from these.[31]

The generation of the Blair sisters has passed. Their artistic talent, sewing skills, hard work, and a glimpse of their living and caring, live on in the records and artifacts they left . . . and in their quilts.


## NOTES

1. Family records compiled by Mary Johnson Browning in the John Blair Estate Collection (JBEC).

2. On the eve of the War Between the States, the average size of a farm in Roane County was between twenty and fifty acres; but many farms were much larger. If the war had not happened, Roane County would have boasted a landed elite. Eugene Monroe Pickel, *A History of Roane County, Tennessee to 1860*, 40.

3. Tax Evaluation, Tenth District, Roane County, 1868 (JBEC).

4. Receipt of purchase of slave "Charly Blair," 1853 (JBEC).

5. Receipt of purchase of slave "Edward," 1863 (JBEC).

6. Conversation with Mary Johnson Browning in Athens, Tennessee, 30 November 1984.

7. On May 6, 1861 the people of Tennessee voted on the questions of secession and representation in the Confederate Congress. The results in Roane County were 454 for and 1568 against separation. Emma Middleton Wells, *The History of Roane County*, 34–35.

8. Conversation with Mary Browning, 2 November 1985.

9. John Blair's name appears as Revenue Commissioner on Tax Evaluation in 1868 (JBEC).

10. Receipt of fees paid for children in Roane County (JBEC).

11. Report of Subjects Taught at Oak Hill School, 1861 (JBEC).

12. Report of School Population in 1868 (JBEC).

13. Ledger sheet of J. Blair at W. J. Betterton, dated 1873 (JBEC).

14. Ledger sheet of Account of J. Blair and S. T. Blair at McEwen and Hornsby, dated 1861 (JBEC).

15. *Comfort*, January, 1900, 1.

16. "Calico Manufacture" *Harper's Bazar*, vol. 1, no. 39, 25 July 1868.

17. Advertisement, *Home Monthly*, January, 1901, 8.

18. Frank V. Williams III, *Pictures of the Past*, 11.

19. Letter from Domestic Sewing Machine Company, Richmond, Tennessee to John Blair, Esq., dated 24 May 1878 (JBEC).

20. Elinor Lander Horwitz, *Mountain People, Mountain Crafts*, 115-116.

21. Sadye Tune Wilson and Doris Finch Kennedy, *Of Coverlets: The Legacies, the Weavers*, 176–177.

22. The blue jean jacket in wool should not be confused with modern day cotton twill jeans.

23. Harriet Blair to Blair sisters, 10 December 1882 (JBEC).

24. Mary Blair to Blair sisters, 9 April 1883 (JBEC).

25. Harriet Blair to Blair sisters, 20 May 1883 (JBEC).

26. Harriet Blair to John Blair and his daughters, 25 January 1885 (JBEC).

27. Mary Blair to John Blair, 25 January 1885 (JBEC).

28. Harriet Blair to Blair sisters, 20 July 1890 (JBEC).

29. Mark H. Taliaferro to Mary Ann Blair, 3 March 1861 (JBEC).

30. Dan Blair to John Edgar Levi Johnson, 27 January 1924 (JBEC).

31. Will of John Edgar Levi Johnson, 22 September 1969 (JBEC).

# *Conclusion*

We have tried in this study of Tennessee quilts to honor the quilt-makers who have enriched the lives of their families with their needlework and left us their legacies. The past—going back 150 years—becomes more real when we touch the work done by a great-grandmother's hands. From her work we gain a better understanding of her life and our appreciation increases.

Quilts provided a conversation point and a beginning as we gathered family histories during the survey. From quilts, stories on many topics unfolded and revealed scenes from earlier times. Some communities which enjoyed a relatively stable population offered rich sources of information. We found instances where household goods remained in a house during several successive generations of a family. In these cases we could readily document the continuity of family life and place the findings in their appropriate historical context. The study became much broader than a mere cataloging of quilts. It was a gathering of human experience.

We were especially pleased to find that most of the quilts documented had remained in the families of the makers. All of the owners expressed a sense of pride in their quilts. Bringing quilts to the survey quickened their interest in history and genealogy. They were pleased to be able to pass on the documentation information related to their quilts and to be more knowledgeable about quilt care. Not all of the present generation has retained the practice of quiltmaking, but perhaps through the study's emphasis on family traditions old lessons may be learned anew.

The study was a beginning. There are still questions unresolved and further research to be done. By posing a few questions, we may be able to find answers and put together more of the puzzle. We offer these mysteries for consideration and invite comments on these and other matters.

Why was East Tennessee, unlike nearby regions, an area where many fine applique quilts were made?

Where did the early nineteenth-century patterns come from?

93

Why was there heavy concentration of stuffed quilts in certain parts of East Tennessee, and why later than in other places?

Are other linsey quilts extant?

What other fund-raising quilts were made for the Confederacy?

Are there other original designs, peddler designs, folk-art inventions?

Are there more slave-made quilts and nineteenth-century quilts made by black women?

Cuesta Benberry, the noted quilt historian, commented on the Tennessee quilt study and similar state research projects in a letter to the authors:

> "The catalogs promise to be *the* major research work of the 1980s. They will, I predict, go down in quilt history as primary research efforts never before attempted. Whatever the selection process, whatever the approach of the Project leaders, the central fact is, they are producing documents built on primary research. When all the projects are done, we are going to take a giant step forward in quilt history information. I am pleased that I am living while the body of work is being compiled."

We, too, are pleased that we have been able to present a segment of American history through the study of Tennessee quilts and their makers.

*Correspondence may be directed to:*

Bets Ramsey
Box 4146
Chattanooga, TN 37405

Merikay Waldvogel
1501 Whitower Road
Knoxville, TN 37919

# *Acknowledgments*

The documentation of Tennessee quilts has been a cooperative venture from its beginning. The generous contributions of hundreds of people made the project possible. Every gesture of support was important and resulted in an impressive collective enterprise.

Primary honors go to the quiltmakers whose spirit is passed on in the legacy of their quilts. They are the ones we celebrate. We are grateful also for their descendants who, through the years, lovingly protected the quilts and the memories of their makers. The quilt owners graciously shared their family treasures and made the exhibition possible. Makers' and lenders' names are acknowledged elsewhere with their quilts.

Advice, consultation and reinforcement have come from Cuesta Benberry, Katy Christopherson, Sally Garoutte, Joyce Gross, Laurel Horton, Julie Silber, Jeannette Lasansky, Shelly Zegart, Suellen Meyer, Muriel Mayfield, Penny Tschantz, Michael Kile, Bettina Havig, Carole Orr, Linda Evans, Shelly Williams, Ruth S. Holmberg, Nina Brock, Betty Duggan and Dena Katzenberg. Barbara Brackman has been especially helpful in clarifying and solving pattern identification problems.

We are deeply indebted to the agents and staff of the United States Agricultural Extension Service of the University of Tennessee District and their Home Demonstration Club members. Our thanks go to Ann Burn, Peggie Hall, Barbara Martin, Juanita Patterson, Elna Spears, Jeanne Webb, Mary Frances Hamilton, Barbara Holt, Martha Marklin, and Mary Theresa Lowry. They coordinated quilt days and performed many valuable services.

Our appreciation also goes to the photographers, who were most willing and able: Melinda Hillman, Linda Claussen, Susan Parks, Joe Duncan, Jan Wilkins, Bob Wright, Betsy Donahue, Peggy Turner, David Vetto, Bob Manis, Jim Cox, and Larry Rhodes. David Luttrell deserves our deep admiration for preparing the book's photographs.

Local quilt coordinators were the key to the success of the Tennessee quilt project. Without compensation they prepared most ably for each quilt day. These coordinators were: Dot Davis, Fay Whelchel, Ben Humphries, Selma Shapiro, Ann Morelock, Rick Ownby, Duay O'Neil, Janet Higgins, Cindy Randals, Mary Granger, Dan Pomeroy, Mary Clemons, Anita McCabe, Frieda Holt, Mildred Locke, Emily Cox, Debbie Harvey, Wanda James, Martha Ferris, Elsie Johnson, Jan Wilkins, and Millie McBride.

Volunteers learned their tasks quickly and willingly gave many hours of service. Local volunteers at each site were:

*Athens:* Jan Wilkins, Sharon Gordon, Lora Creasman, Louise Haney, Dora Scheer, Ann Chittenden, Faye Chittenden, Melinda Hillman, and Linda Claussen.

*Bell Buckle:* Elsie Whitaker, Mildred Locke, Joyce Cole, Gerry Williams, Fred Williams, Marvin Whitaker, Barbara Landis, Peggy Bell, Mary Cross, Sibyl Steiner, and Juanita Patterson.

*Chattanooga:* Fay Whelchel, Lorraine Timmons, Anne Nolan, Esther Barnwell, Dot Davis, Billie Salmons, Susan Parks, Joe Duncan, Marcia Hall, Margaret Coffey, Bobbie Fant, Catherine Blevins, Nellie Mae Rankin, Betsy Donahue, and Bob Wright.

*Clarksville:* Martha Marklin, Susan Elliott, Marion Campbell, Evelyn Morrison, Frieda Holt, Jenny Corp, Faye Perkins, Janie Karrigan, Carlena Hatcher, Jewell Hundley, Virginia Uetz, Vicki Dean, Dan Ross, and Dorothy Ross.

*Cleveland:* Ann Morelock, Barbara Edwards, Joan E. Barrett, Mary R. Keasler, Linda Claussen, Ann Rabun, Kathy Heeter, Marcia Hall, Melinda Hillman, Jan Wilkins, Dora Scheer, Jeanne Driese, Kay Cummings, Ann Chittenden, and Juanita England.

*Crossville:* Ann Burn, Mary Frances Hamilton, Bettye Sloan, June Prett, Judy Smith, Amy Hart, Lora Creasman, and Louise Haney.

*Dayton:* Peggie Hall, Nelle Chattiro, Henrietta Tallent, Florence Crosby, Mattie Crosby, Blanche Starring, Eloise Panozzo, Cornelia Halliday, Shirley Swearingen, Nancy Kellogg, Esther Barnwell, Dot Davis, Nellie Diehl, Imogene Crosby, Vista Mahan, Susan Parks, Carolyn Koster, and Carolyn Whitley.

*Gatlinburg:* Ben Humphries, Sandy Graham, Jeanne Driese, Johnnie McGaha, Grace L. Clabo, Hazel Hembree, Sue Whitney, Mary Kay King, Jo Weir, Olin Watson, and Sidney Weeter.

*Greeneville:* Martha Ferris, Mary Granger, Linda Claussen, Jo Ellen Hale, Bertha Harmon, Charlotte Stollard, Nell Rader, Jane McGehee, Karol Lynn Johnson, Eva Earle Kent, Sandy Cartwright, Rebecca Booker, Barbara Holt, Paul McClure, Arnold Hunter, and Harry Roberts.

*Jonesborough:* Mary Granger, Polly B. Taylor, Evelyn Doak, Jane McGehee, Gladys Lady, Ane Martin, Karol Lynn Johnson, Jo Ellen Hale, Melinda Hillman, Jan Wilkins, and Linda Claussen.

*Knoxville:* Mary Ann Handel, Jane Pearce, Rob Pearce, Mary Lynn Majors, Penny Tschantz, Jeanne Driese, and Melinda Hillman.

*Manchester:* Jeanne Webb, Cuba Ashburn, Barbara Knox, Jamie Phillips, Annie Ruth Norvell, Marjorie Anderson, and Mary Jane Thomas.

*Memphis:* Wanda James, Debbie Harvey, Teresa Bowling, Mary Montgomery, Edna Bomar, Kaaren Reid, and Jewel Rosenberg.

*Murfreesboro:* Jan Higgins, Pat Neal, Dona Vickrey, Joy Carol Anthony, Ed Anthony, Diana Cushing, Melinda Hillman, Susan Parks, Sandra Parker, Westy and William Windham, Virginia Shinn, Sue Miller, Martha Mankin, Margaret Dismukes, Mary Ann Cosity, Margaret Barb, Sam Ella Weatherly, Corkie Myers, Jenn Myers, Virginia Shinn, and Lois West.

*Nashville:* Elsie Johnson, Al Johnson, Kathryn Tramel, Barbara Sandvig, Eleanor Swanborg, Miriam Dabbs, Doris Northington, Joyce Cole, Barbara Prichard, Jenny Moss, Virginia Taylor, Linda Cartwright, Emily Daniel Cox, Dot Arnold, Elizabeth Bowman, Linda Claussen, Pat Neal, and June Dorman.

*Newport:* Duay O'Neil, Linda Claussen, and Penny Tschantz.

*Oak Ridge:* Jeanne Driese, Penny Tschantz, Suzanne Tumblin, Bob Manis, Peggy Turner, Mary Lynn Majors, and Linda Claussen.

*Paris:* Emily Daniel Cox, Jim Cox, Larry Rhodes, Letitia Covington, Myrtle Fuller, Kay Richardson, Ruth Reynolds, Dell Caldwell, Marian Buckley, Betty Hudson, Shellie Parker, Dianna Maddox, Debra Lee Davenport, Anita Peale, Lina Nash, Linda Black, Laura Fuller, Brenda Fuller, Louis Stoope, Barbara Lynn Cagle, and Ruth Reisentz.

*Pulaski:* Anita McCabe, Helen Clark, Mary Alice Story, Barbara Jennings, Margaret Jackson, Mary Lee Harris, Mary Theresa Lowry, Lavonia Mansfield, Mabel H. Martin, and Billie Aymett.

*Shelbyville:* Juanita Patterson, Sibyl Steiner, Brownie McNabb, Ann Throneberry, Mildred Locke, Elma Denton, Mattie Ray Wiser, Catherine Talley, Katie Pickle, Gladys Papa, Sue Archer, Irene Marlin, and Loretta Sparn.

*Silver Dollar City:* Linda Claussen, Melinda Hillman, Mary Ann Handel, Mark Handel, Jeanne Driese, Willie Atchley, Jean Lester, and Penny Tschantz.

*Sweetwater/Vonore:* Sherry Landers and Linda Claussen.

*Winchester:* Mary Clemons, Leona Ashby, Debbie Ashby, Edna Conway, Lillian Finchum, Agnes Smartt, Sandy Blake, Geraldine Syler, Mary Rich, Meredith Anne Simmons, Sherryl Ezell, Robert W. Clemons, Mary Ruth Simmons, Jeanne Sinclair, Shirley McDonald, Grillis Sinclair, Lucy Hollis, Elna Spears, Suzanne Eades, Barbara Williams, Barbara Clark, William Clemons, and Diane Jones.

Contributions for survey expenses, speakers' fees, and donations came from Silver Dollar City, Gatlinburg Chamber of Commerce, the Hunter Museum of Art, the Children's Museum of Oak Ridge, Fine Arts Committee and Women's History Week Committee of Middle Tennessee State University, Tennessee Valley Quilters' Association, Booneslick Trail (Missouri) Quilters' Guild, Western North Carolina Quilters' Guild, Mrs. Bachman Hodge, Mrs. John Soper, Mr. Neal Coulter, Dogwood Arts Festival of Knoxville, Quilt Guild of Paris, and Nathanael Greene Museum.

These funds were augmented by donations from quilt owners who received copies of their quilts' documentations and made possible the taking of hundreds of slides and photographs at quilt days. For this we are most grateful.

We are indebted to the directors and staffs of those institutions and centers where quilt days were held. Their facilities were pleasant, and their personnel accommodating. Our thanks go to: McMinn County Living Heritage Museum, the Hunter Museum of Art, Senior Neighbors of Chattanooga, Inc., Pi Beta Phi Elementary School, the Children's Museum of Oak Ridge, Cleveland State Community College, the University of Tennessee at Knoxville, Silver Dollar City, Newport-Cocke County Museum, Middle Tennessee State University, Jonesborough Visitors' Center, Tennessee State Museum, 100 Oaks Castle, Pulaski Union Bank, Hilldale Methodist Church of Clarksville, Shelbyville Farm Bureau Building, Middle Tennessee Electric Building, Duck River Electric Building, Bell Buckle Community Center, Henry County Farm Bureau Building, Memphis College of Arts, St. John's Lutheran Church of Donelson, Clyde M. York 4-H Training Center, Rhea County Courthouse, and the Nathanael Greene Museum.

The Hunter Museum of Art has been our protector and guardian. We are grateful for the confidence of its director, Cleve Scarbrough. For all the staff members who gave their assistance, especially Kay Morris, William Henning, Beth O'Leary, and Tim Flick, we have high professional respect.

An able advisory committee—Linda Claussen, Veronica Fitzgerald, Jane McElroy, Linda Evans, and Sandra Cartwright—reviewed numerous quilt slides before making exhibition recommendations.

Funding for preparation of the publication and exhibition was provided by supporting institutions: the Hunter Museum of Art, the American Museum of Science and Energy, The Parthenon, the Carroll Reece Museum, the Rose Center of Morristown, The Knoxville Museum of Art, and the Memphis Pink Palace Museum, Nathanael Greene Museum, Greeneville, and the following companies and individuals:

*Patron:* Whittle Communications, Knoxville, Tennessee

*Friends:* Ruth S. and A. William Holmberg; Mayfield Dairy Farms, Inc., Athens, Tennessee, Lea-Wayne Knitting Mills, Morristown.

*Sponsors:* Arlene Garrison in memory of Sarah Jane Longbottom Davidson and Sadie Ethel Brown Morton; Lorene Mantooth; Mississippi Delta Railroad; Quilter's Haven; Marilyn Rogers in memory of Laura Archer; Hibbard Thatcher in appreciation to Ruby Thatcher; Mr. and Mrs. Forrest I. Watson; Smoky Mountain Quilters; an anonymous sponsor.

*Contributors:* Sandra Cartwright; Mrs. Harold Cash; "For Women Only," Hixson First Baptist Church; Wanda Jenkins in memory of Estelle Peters Hyden; Dan and Mayna MacKinnon; Mr. and Mrs. Ward W. Miller in honor of June Winter Miller; Dr. Philip J. More; Mr. and Mrs. Paul Neely; Roberta B. Parrish; Dick and Alice Ramsey; Pauline Spencer in honor of Julia Alice Gobble McMahan; Al Waldvogel and family in memory of Helen Tasa Waldvogel; several anonymous contributors.

*Donors:* Esther Barnwell in memory of Margaret Coffey; Linda Cartwright in honor of Elsie Johnson; Chattanooga Quilters' Guild; Herb and Sue Cohn; Mrs. Whitney Colburn; Florence Crosby; Barbara Hale in honor of Barbara Ford Tunnell; Rhoda Heiskell; Almeda Hood Hill; Mrs. John Hodges in memory of Nell Hodges; Mrs. William G. Knight in memory of Mrs. John Morehead; Dr. and Mrs. Michael Kosanovich; Ellen McReynolds in memory of Bess Collins McReynolds and Mary Bates McReynolds; McMinn County Living Heritage Museum; Gay McNemer; Ann Morelock; Ellen Morgan in memory of Eliza Benton Bagley; Julia Needham; Anne Nolan; Polly's Antiques of Greeneville; Mrs. Martha L. Shelton; Mrs. Florence B. Striegel; Betty Stroud; Mary Elizabeth Suiter as "a tribute to the beauty within these women which shines forth through their quilts"; Sarah Thomas; Peggy Turner; Mary Wasson in memory of Victoria Darwin Caldwell; Norma L. Bagley in honor of Mildred Locke; Jeanne G. Webb in memory of Belle M. Gilmore; Carolyn Whitley in honor of Blanche Conley Young; Nelle Mae Rankin in memory of Margaret Coffey; Mary L. Neusel; Mary Granger and William and Westy Windham; Elizabeth P. Bowman in honor of Sudie D. Pepper.

Our apologies go to anyone inadvertently omitted. You have our thanks.

Paul Ramsey and Sarah Farmer offered valuable editorial assistance, and Jerry Ledbetter gave encouragement. Very special thanks go to Mrs. David G. Stone who led us to a pleasant association with Rutledge Hill Press.

As for ourselves, we set out with an adventurous spirit and, with no adequate funding, had the faith and courage to carry out the project. We managed to maintain harmony and humor in the most difficult situations, and we are still friends. Our gratitude is extended to each one who had a part in this study of Tennessee quilts.

[**90**] LINSEY QUILT.

*Maker:* Unknown.
  Found in Knox County, circa 1850.
*Lender:* Jerry Ledbetter.
*Pieced:* 79″ x 63¼″; wool: navy, brown,
  pink, handwoven fabric; blue and red
  handwoven back; binding is front to
  back; quilting is diagonal rows 1½″
  apart.

The quilt is made of garment scraps of
linsey, a handwoven cloth made of wool
and cotton. The blue fabric, which looks
similar to the modern-day blue jean fabric
but much coarser, was used in men's
jackets and trousers. The striped and
checked fabrics were often used in women's
skirts. The cloth is known as linsey because
it originally had linen as the warp thread;
however, linsey fabric is often found with
cotton for the warp.

# Glossary

*Applique:* laid-on pieces of cloth sewed to a background material.

*Backing:* material used as the underside of the quilt.

*Batt:* a small unit of cotton or wool filler combed by hand or wire brushes called cards. Also factory-made in a single sheet.

*Batting:* the padding or filler of a quilt.

*Binding:* finish for the raw edge of the quilt, done with a strip of straight or bias material.

*Block:* a unit or section of a quilt made of joined pieces or of background material with applied pieces.

*Border:* solid, pieced, or appliqued band at outer edge of quilt or surrounding center medallion.

*Broderie perse:* "Persian embroidery," cutout applique designs usually of cotton chintz, sometimes combined with pieced work, especially eighteenth and early nineteenth centuries.

*Cambric:* a glazed cotton cloth which is paper thin. An old spelling is "cambrick."

*Carding:* combing the cotton or wool with wire brushes to prepare it for spinning or for quilt filler.

*Comfort:* a tied quilt.

*Crazy:* irregular shapes usually joined with embroidery stitches.

*Design:* the overall organization of a quilt, or a specific pattern.

*Domestic:* an old name for muslin cloth.

*Elbow Quilting:* allover design of concentric arc rows of quilting. The elbow can act as a compass point in drawing the major arc.

*Fan Quilting:* (see preceding entry).

*Filling:* the padding of a quilt, usually cotton or wool, placed between the top and bottom fabric of the quilt.

*Flax:* the plant from which linen thread is spun.

*Frame* (or quilting frame): basically four strips of wood in rectangular shape to which is fastened the three layers of the quilt prior to quilting.

*Linsey:* a shortened form for linsey-woolsey, a fabric once woven of linen and wool. In Tennessee in the nineteenth century it was more often made of cotton and wool.

*Medallion:* quilt with large center motif surrounded by borders or other units.

*Pattern:* the design unit of a quilt, most designs being traditional.

*Patchwork:* pieces of fabric seamed together, as in pieced work, or applied to a background, as in applique, and joined together to make a whole.

*Pieced Work:* joining pieces by seaming together to make a whole, usually in geometric design.

*Quilt:* two layers of cloth with padding between, stitched or tied together.

*Quilting:* stitching through layers of fabric and padding.

*Sashing:* band added between blocks in joining.

*Set:* the material used, as well as the arrangement of joining blocks.

*Shell Quilting:* (see Elbow Quilting).

*Skein:* a coil of spun yarn or thread.

*String Piecing:* the joining of narrow strips of fabric, usually in random size, to make a unit.

*Stuffed Work:* the addition of extra filler to quilted or appliqued designs to make a raised surface.

*Template Piecing:* a method of basting under the edges of fabric shapes to paper shapes and joining the edges of the units together with whip-stitches. Frequently used for hexagons.

*Top:* the upper and outer layer of a quilt.

*Warp:* the threads running lengthwise in a loom when weaving cloth.

*Weft:* the yarn carried across the warp when weaving cloth.

*Whitework:* a quilt with a top of solid white embellished with quilting.

*Wholecloth:* quilt top of solid material, often three panels seamed together and quilted.

# *Museums*

A questionaire was sent to Tennessee's museums and historical homes requesting information about quilts in their collections. The following institutions responded. We urge Tennesseans to visit these museums and to consider donating their family quilts should they decide to part with them.

## EAST TENNESSEE

ARROWMONT SCHOOL
P.O. Box 567
Gatlinburg 37738
615-436-5860

Quilts are included in invitational and competitive exhibitions.

CARROLL REECE MUSEUM
P.O. Box 22,300A
East Tennessee State University
Johnson City 37614
615-929-4392

Nineteenth and twentieth century regional quilts are included in the collection. One has an embroidered top; another is a Dutch Doll pattern; one is a wallhanging made by a local quilters' guild. Both patchwork and applique techniques are represented. An annual exhibition.

CHILDREN'S MUSEUM OF OAK RIDGE
461 West Outer Drive
Oak Ridge 37716
615-482-1074

Collection includes twenty Tennessee quilts of various patterns. Two were possibly made circa 1850. Condition fine to worn.

CRAVENS HOUSE, NATIONAL PARK SERVICE
Point Park, Lookout Mountain 37350
615-821-7786

Six quilts are displayed in bedrooms of an historic house which served in turn as Confederate and Union headquarters during the War Between the States.

GREAT SMOKY MOUNTAINS NATIONAL PARK
Gatlinburg 37738
615-436-1295

Four quilts are exhibited on beds in the Cable House at Cades Cove. Open April to November each year.

HOUSTON ANTIQUE MUSEUM
201 High Street
Chattanooga 37403
615-267-7176

A small collection of quilts and coverlets can be seen during museum hours.

HUNTER MUSEUM OF ART
10 Bluff View
Chattanooga 37403
615-267-0968

Annual invitational exhibitions of antique and contemporary quilts are shown in April and May. No significant holdings at present.

JONESBOROUGH-WASHINGTON COUNTY HISTORY MUSEUM
P.O. Box 451
Jonesborough 37959
615-753-9775

A friendship quilt presented to John S. Mathes by the Ladies of Jonesborough, December 15, 1860.

FRANK H. McCLUNG MUSEUM
University of Tennessee
Circle Park Drive
Knoxville 37996
615-974-2144

Museum collection includes five quilts, most of which were made in Tennessee from 1821-1900. To view the quilts, contact the Curator of Collections.

MCMINN COUNTY LIVING HERITAGE MUSEUM
P.O. Box 889
Athens 37303
615-745-0329

Some twelve quilts exhibited on a rotating basis are owned by the museum, and several others on loan are exhibited regularly. Most of these quilts were made in the late 1800s and early 1900s and were donated to the museum from local families. Many are examples of very fine workmanship and are in relatively good condition.

NEWPORT-COCKE COUNTY MUSEUM
P.O. Box 246
Mulberry Street
Newport 37821
615-623-7304

Approximately twenty-five quilts are exhibited at various times. All quilts in the collection were probably made in Cocke County. Most are traditional patterns made between 1900 and 1930, although a few quilts date from the mid-1870s. To make an appointment to see the quilts call 615-623-7304 (Community Center), and they will call museum staff.

RED CLAY STATE HISTORIC PARK
Route #6 Box 306
Cleveland 37311
615-472-2627

Collection includes twenty-five quilts, which are exhibited several at a time on a rotating basis. Twenty-two small quilts were made within the past ten years in Bradley County for the museum to demonstrate historical patterns. Three appliqued and embroidered quilts from the late nineteenth century were made at various places in the Southeast. All are displayed in the context of daily life of the nineteenth century Cherokee Indians. Special arrangements can be made to view the entire collection by contacting the Park Manager.

## MIDDLE TENNESSEE

AUSTIN PEAY STATE UNIVERSITY—ART DEPT.
P.O. Box 4677
Clarksville 37044
615-648-3348

The Trahern Art Gallery at Austin Peay State University has no quilt in its university art collection, but has held occasional exhibits of antique quilts from this region.

THE CARTER HOUSE A.P.T.A.
1140 Columbia Avenue
Franklin 37064
615-791-1861

Some twelve quilts all made in Williamson County, Franklin, Tennessee, dating from early 1800 to 1886. Quilts may be seen by appointment or on regular tours of the Carter House.

CLARKSVILLE-MONTGOMERY COUNTY HISTORICAL
   MUSEUM
200 S. Second Street
P.O. Box 383
Clarksville 37040
615-645-2507

Twelve quilts, dating from the nineteenth century to the first quarter of the twentieth century, exhibited three months yearly. Special group arrangements can be made to view the entire collection by contacting the museum.

THE HERMITAGE
4580 Rachel's Lane
Hermitage 37076
615-889-2941

Quilts from the family of Andrew Jackson are displayed on the beds in this National Registered Historic Landmark.

MUSEUM OF TOBACCO ART AND HISTORY
800 Harrison Street
Nashville 37203
615-242-9218

The museum has two silk cigar ribbon quilts and a matching pillow sham in its collection. The quilts and sham are made from hundreds of silk cigar ribbons that were once wrapped around bundles of cigars. One of the quilts was made near Boston, Massachusetts; it is on permanent display.

OAKLANDS HISTORIC HOUSE MUSEUM
900 North Maney Avenue
Murfreesboro 37130
615-893-0022

Three quilts, two having stuffed work; the third is a crazy quilt. All are believed to have been made in Middle Tennessee. The quilts are exhibited in period room settings.

OSCAR FARRIS AGRICULTURAL MUSEUM
Ellington Agricultural Center
P.O. Box 40627
Nashville 37204
615-360-0197

Four quilts from the Gambill family of Mountain City, dating from 1885 are on permanent display. Also one string quilt made in the early part of the twentieth century from the Farris family is included in the museum. A Log Cabin quilt pieced in the 1950s is in frames and everyone who visits the museum is invited to join in quilting. Other quilts are displayed occasionally.

TENNESSEE STATE MUSEUM
505 Dederick Street
Nashville, TN 37219
615-741-2692

The collection of quilts at the Tennessee State Museum includes over 100 quilts. Most of the quilts in the collection are of Tennessee origin. The quilts date from 1800 to 1986 and are of a wide variety of patterns including an early stuffed and chintz quilt. Currently fifteen quilts are on display in the quilt gallery on the lower floor of the museum. In 1989 the number on exhibit will increase to 25 or more quilts which will be rotated on a yearly basis. Arrangements to study the quilts in storage can be made through the Curator of Fashion and Textiles.

UPPER ROOM MUSEUM
1908 Grand Avenue
Nashville 37202
615-327-2700

Museum has two quilts on display, one of which belonged to Elisha Carr (1806–1866), who was a circuit rider with the Methodist Church in Tennessee. The other quilt made by Genoa Smith has thirty crosses in red on a white background (date unknown).

SAM DAVIS HOME
Sam Davis Highway
Smyrna 37167
615-459-2341

Collection includes thirteen quilts, most of which are on permanent display. One quilt called ''The Reel'' was made by Sam Davis's mother and grandmother for him. The makers of the other twelve are unknown but thought to be Tennesseans. The collection includes pieced, applique and crazy quilt designs and are done in cottons, wools and silks. All are examples of fine craftsmanship and most are in excellent condition.

OLD JAIL MUSEUM
400 First Avenue NE
Winchester 37398
615-967-0524

Three quilts made in Franklin County, Tennessee, seventy-five to one hundred years ago are on display in the museum when it is open. No appointment is necessary to see the quilts.

## WEST TENNESSEE

CENTER FOR SOUTHERN FOLKLORE
1216 Peabody
Memphis 38104
901-726-4205

Collection consists of contemporary Afro-American quilts made in 1960s and 1970s by Pecolia Warner from Yazoo City, Mississippi and ten quilts made in 1930s and 1940s as a project of the Memphis Park Commission.

MAGEVNEY HOUSE
198 Adams
Memphis 38103
901-526-4464

MEMPHIS PINK PALACE MUSEUM
3050 Central Avenue
Memphis 38111
901-454-5600

Some thirteen quilts in collections, of which several including a baby quilt from 1790s are on display in History of Memphis exhibit. Several are also on display in room settings at branch facility Magevney House. Most quilts in collections date from mid-nineteenth through early twentieth century and probably were made in mid-south or southeast. Qualified researchers may view quilts in storage by prior arrangement with Chief Curator of Collections.

[**91**] Detail of number 66, page 65.

# Bibliography

Allen, Gloria Seaman. *Old Line Traditions: Maryland Women and Their Quilts.* Washington, D.C.: DAR Museum, 1985.

Beer, Alice Baldwin. *Trade Goods: A Study of Indian Chintz.* Washington, D.C.: The Smithsonian Institution, 1970.

Beyer, Jinny. *The Scrap Look.* McLean, Virginia: EPM Publications, Inc., 1985.

Binney, Edwin, and Gail Binney-Winslow. *Homage to Amanda.* San Francisco: R. F. Press, 1984.

Brackman, Barbara. "Dating Old Quilts." *Quilter's Newsletter Magazine.* Issues 165–169.

———. *An Encyclopedia of Pieced Quilt Patterns.* 8 vols. Lawrence, Kansas: Prairie Flower Publishing, 1979–1983.

Brett, Gerard. *European Printed Textiles.* London: His Majesty's Stationery Office, 1949.

Bullard, Lacy Folmar, and Betty Jo Shiell. *Chintz Quilts: Unfading Glory.* Tallahassee, Florida: Serendipity Publishers, 1983.

Cargo, Robert, Gail C. Andrews, and Janet Strain McDonald. *Black Belt to Hill Country: Alabama Quilts from the Robert and Helen Cargo Collection.* Birmingham, Alabama: Birmingham Museum of Art, 1982.

Clarke, Mary Washington. *Kentucky Quilts and Their Makers.* Lexington, Kentucky: The University of Kentucky Press, 1976.

Colby, Averil. *Patchwork.* 1958. Reprint. London: B. T. Batsford Ltd., 1983.

———. *Patchwork Quilts.* 1965. Reprint. London: B. T. Batsford Ltd., 1975.

———. *Quilting.* New York: Charles Scribner's Sons, 1971.

Cooper, Patricia and Norma Bradley Buferd. *The Quilters: Women and Domestic Art.* Garden City, New York: Anchor Press, 1978.

Dubois, Jean. *A Galaxy of Stars: America's Favorite Quilts.* Durango, Colorado: La Plata Press, 1976.

Dunton, William Rush, Jr. *Old Quilts.* Cantonsville, Maryland: privately printed, 1946.

Eaton, Allen H. *Handicrafts of the Southern Highlands: A Book on Rural Arts.* New York: Russell Sage Foundation, 1937.

Edwards, Phoebe. *The Mountain Mist Blue Book of Quilts.* Cincinnati: Stearns & Foster, no date.

Elwood, Judy, Joyce Tennery, and Alice Richardson. *Tennessee Quilting: Designs Plus Patterns.* Oak Ridge: privately printed, 1982.

Finley, Ruth E. *Old Patchwork Quilts and the Women Who Made Them,* 1929. Reprint. Newton Center, Massachusetts: Charles T. Branford Co., 1970.

Fox, Sandi. *Small Endearments: Nineteenth-Century Quilts for Children*. New York: Charles Scribner's Sons, 1985.

Freeman, Roland. *Something to Keep You Warm*. Jackson, Mississippi: Mississippi Department of Archives and History, 1981.

Frye, L. Thomas, ed. *American Quilts: A Handmade Legacy*. Oakland, California: The Oakland Museum, 1981.

Garoutte, Sally, ed. *Uncoverings*. Mill Valley, California: American Quilt Study Group, 1980–1984.

Gutcheon, Beth. *The Perfect Patchwork Primer*. New York: David McKay Co., Inc., 1973.

Haders, Phyllis. *The Warner Collectors' Guide to American Quilts*. New York: Warner Books, Main Street Press, 1981.

Hall, Carrie A., and Rose G. Kretsinger. *The Romance of the Patchwork Quilt in America*. New York: Bonanza Books, 1935.

Holstein, Jonathan. *The Pieced Quilt: An American Design Tradition*. Greenwich, Connecticut: New York Graphic Society, Ltd., 1973.

Horwitz, Elinor Lander. *Mountain People, Mountain Crafts*. Philadelphia: J. B. Lippincott Co., 1974.

Horton, Laurel. "South Carolina Quilts in the Civil War." Forthcoming *Uncoverings 1985*. Edited by Sally Garoutte. Mill Valley, California: American Quilt Study Group, [1986].

Horton, Laurel, and Lynn Robertson Myers, eds. *Social Fabric: South Carolina's Traditional Quilts*. Columbia, South Carolina: McKissick Museum, University of South Carolina, no date.

Ickis, Marguerite. *The Standard Book of Quilt Making and Collecting*, 1949. Reprint. New York: Dover Publications, Inc., 1959.

Irwin, John Rice. *A People and Their Quilts*. Exton, Pennsylvania: Schiffer Publishing Ltd., 1983.

Johnson, Mary Elizabeth. *A Garden of Quilts*. Birmingham, Alabama: Oxmoor House, Inc., 1984.

Katzenberg, Dena. *Baltimore Album Quilts*. Baltimore: The Baltimore Museum of Art, 1981.

Kentucky Quilt Project. *Kentucky Quilts 1800–1900*. Louisville, Kentucky: The Kentucky Quilt Project, Inc., 1982.

Kolter, Jane Bentley. *Forget Me Not: A Gallery of Friendship and Album Quilts*. Pittstown, New Jersey: The Main Street Press, 1985.

Lasansky, Jeannette. *In the Heart of Pennsylvania: 19th and 20th Century Quiltmaking Traditions*. Lewisburg, Pennsylvania: Oral Traditions Project of the Union County Historical Society, 1985.

Lipsett, Linda Otto. *Remember Me: Women and Their Friendship Quilts*. San Francisco: The Quilt Digest Press, 1985.

McKendry, Ruth. *Traditional Quilts and Bed Coverings*. New York: Van Nostrand Reinhold Company, 1979.

McKim, Ruby S. *101 Patchwork Patterns*. 2nd ed. New York: Dover Publications, Inc., 1962.

McMorris, Penny. *Crazy Quilts*. New York: E. P. Dutton, Inc., 1984.

Malone, Maggie. *1001 Patchwork Designs*. New York: Sterling Publishing Co., Inc., 1982.

Marshall, Martha. *Quilts of Appalachia: The Mountain Woman and Her Quilts*. Bluff City, Tennessee: Tri-City Printing Co., 1972.

Mills, Susan Winter. *Illustrated Index to Traditional American Quilt Patterns*. New York: Arco Publishing, Inc., 1980.

Montgomery, Florence M. *Textiles in America, 1650–1870*. New York: W. W. Norton & Co., 1984.

Newman, Joyce Joines. *North Carolina Country Quilts*. Chapel Hill, North Carolina: The Ackland Art Museum, University of North Carolina at Chapel Hill, 1978.

Nichols, Pat. "String Quilts." In *Uncoverings 1982*. Mill Valley, California: American Quilt Study Group, 1983.

Nylander, Jane D. *Fabrics for Historic Buildings*. Washington, D.C.: The Preservation Press, 1983.

Orlofsky, Patsy and Myron Orlofsky. *Quilts in America*. New York: McGraw-Hill Book Co., 1974.

Patten, Cartter. *A Tennessee Chronicle*. Privately printed, 1953.

Peto, Florence. *American Quilts and Coverlets*. New York: Chanticleer Press Inc., 1949.

———. *Historic Quilts*. New York: The American Historical Company, Inc., 1939.

Pettit, Florence H. *America's Printed and Painted Fabrics*. New York: Hastings House, Publishers, 1970.

Pickel, Eugene Monroe. *A History of Roane County, Tennessee to 1860*. Kingston, Tennessee: The Roane County Heritage Commission, 1981.

Pottinger, David. *Quilts from the Indiana Amish*. New York: E. P. Dutton, Inc., 1983.

Puckett, Marjorie. *String Quilts 'n Things*. Orange, California: Orange Patchwork Publishers, 1979.

Ramsey, Bets, ed. *Quilt Close-Up: Five Southern Views*. Chattanooga, Tennessee: The Hunter Museum of Art, 1983.

———. "The Quilter," *Chattanooga Times*, 17 March 1983.

Ring, Betty, ed. *Needlework: An Historical Survey*. Rev. ed. Pittstown, New Jersey: The Main Street Press, 1984.

Safford, Carleton L., and Robert Bishop. *America's Quilts and Coverlets*. New York: E. P. Dutton & Co., Inc., 1972.

Sienkiewicz, Elly. *Spoken Without a Word*. Washington, D.C.: The Turtle Hill Press, 1983.

Wells, Emma Middleton. *The History of Roane County, Vol. 1*. Chattanooga, Tennessee: Lookout Publishing Company, 1927.

White, Margaret. *Quilts and Counterpanes in the Newark Museum*. New Jersey: The Newark Museum, 1948.

Williams, Frank V., III, *Pictures of the Past*. Rev. ed. Kingston, Tennessee: Roane County Heritage Commission, 1984.

Wilson, Sadye Tune, and Doris Finch Kennedy. *Of Coverlets: The Legacies, the Weavers*. Nashville, Tennessee: Tunstede, 1983.

Yabsley, Suzanne. *Texas Quilts, Texas Women*. College Station, Texas: Texas A & M University Press, 1984.

[**92**] Detail of number 10, page 12.

111

**Boldface** indicates color illustration.